Steven Raichlen's
Guide to
Boston Restaurants

A good meal makes a man feel more charitable
toward the world than any sermon.

Arthur Pendenys

Steven Raichlen's
Guide to
Boston Restaurants
Including Cape Cod, suburbs,
and surrounding areas

Steven Raichlen

A Terry Catchpole Book

The Lewis Publishing Company
Lexington, Massachusetts
Brattleboro, Vermont

First Edition

Text copyright © 1983 by The Lewis Publishing Company

This book is manufactured in the United States of America. It is designed by Dixie Clark, typeset by Neil W. Kelley, and published by The Lewis Publishing Company, Fessenden Road, Brattleboro, Vermont 05301.

Library of Congress Cataloging in Publication Data

Raichlen, Steven.
   Steven Raichlen's Guide to Boston restaurants.

  "A Terry Catchpole book."
   1. Boston (Mass.)—Restaurants—Directories.
2. Restaurants, lunch rooms, etc.—Massachusetts.
I. Title.   II. Title: Guide to Boston restaurants.
TX907.R28   1983   647'.9574461   83–19534
ISBN 0–86616–031–0 (pbk.)

PUBLISHED NOVEMBER 1983
Second printing December 1983
Third printing May 1984

This book is dedicated to Anne Willan and Mark Cherniavsky,
who taught me the art of eating.

CONTENTS

ACKNOWLEDGMENTS

This book would not have been written without the help, advice, and support of many people. My first thanks go to staff and readers of *Boston Magazine* for making my career as a restaurant critic possible. I would also like to thank my editor, Terry Catchpole; my agent, Helen Rees; and my editor at *Boston Magazine*, John Brady; for their patience and expert guidance. Barbara Fitzpatrick, Linda Wong, and Brooks Vedder had the thankless task of fact-checking, proofreading, and editing. Ken Wong often rescued the manuscript from the hungry maws of my computer. Naturally, responsibility for any errors is my own.

A list of the friends and associates who helped with the actual research for this book would be incomplete without the names of Don Balcom, Alison Banks, Karen Biow, Robert Brody, Kate Broughton, Liz Cooney, Shirley Drevich, Sara Eddy, Bob and Ildri Ginn, Katherine Kenney, Nadine Krasnow, Sam Lasoff, Margot LaStrange, Susan Levin, Janet Meakin, Cronin Minton, Tom Price, John Reardon, Sandy Sweetnam, Ted Spach, Andrew Stern, Ken Winokur, and Ted Wroblewsky. Phil Helfaer has my thanks for his spiritual support; Dale Koppel, for providing me an opportunity to share my restaurant experiences with classes at the Main Course.

Finally, an especially grand thanks to the chefs and restaurateurs who have provided me with hundreds of hours of happy eating; to my parents, who took me to my first restaurants; and especially to Barbara Klein ("Miss Miami"), who was there when I could eat or write no more.

> "If I'd a' knowed what a trouble it was to make a book I
> wouldn't 'a' tackled it, and ain't a-going to no more."

> —Mark Twain from *The Adventures of Huckleberry Finn*

THE RESTAURANT CRITIC'S LAMENT

It is 11 o'clock on a typical Friday evening. In the past five days I have breakfasted on eggs Benedict, lunched on linguini, dined on roast duckling, and midnight snacked on Szechuan stir-fry. I have eaten raw fish at a sushi bar, had my tongue blistered by North Indian curry, and compared cream cheese brownies at two fiercely rivalrous sweet shops. I have endured the indignities of over-priced drinks, haughty waiters, cold steaks, canned whipped cream, and watery coffee. I have eaten out at 11 restaurants in 5 days, and, believe me, at the moment I feel awful.

As restaurant critic for *Boston Magazine*, I probably have one of the most envied jobs in the city. Yet, much as working in restaurant dining rooms sure beats punching a time clock or commuting to the office, the eat-for-pay profession does have its pitfalls. To dine out once or twice a week for pleasure is very different than dining out as often as ten times a week for the purpose of reviewing restaurants. Obliged to try the best the chef has to offer, I make a steady diet of fancified, cream-rich house specialties, while secretly longing for a steak and potato. While other customers eat, drink, and make merry, I scribble furtively on my note pad. (If you want to pass yourself off as a restaurant critic, try taking notes during your meal.) All of which would be fine if my meals were extraordinary, but 70 percent of the time they are not.

As a rule my restaurant visits take place anonymously. (I use a variety of pseudonyms, and take pains to keep my back to the kitchen.) My reviews are based on an average of four meals at a restaurant—usually accomplished by two visits with a party of two. To give the restaurateur a second chance, I almost always return to the scene of the crime, when I have had a bad experience, and when deadline or budget constraints (or sheer lack of courage) prevent a return visit, to be fair, I say so in print. Generally it is I (or *Boston Magazine*), not the restaurant, who pays for my meals and those of my companions. This is the only way to avoid preferential treatment, and it frees me to speak my mind without obligation to the proprietor. My friends and associates accompany me to restaurants, and all are used to playing "musical plates" to enable me to sample a maximum number of dishes on the menu.

Unlike most restaurant reviewers I was a practicing chef before I became a critic. I attended the Cordon Bleu and La Varenne cooking schools in Paris, and have worked in restaurants in France and in this country. (I still teach cooking classes.) I like to think that my practical cooking experience makes me a more knowledgeable critic; it certainly makes me a more sympathetic one. I prefer to write good reviews rather than bad ones, to tell the people about exciting new places rather than about over-rated spots to avoid. Nonetheless, I will not hesitate to blast a bad restaurant, particularly if it charges high prices. I believe that a good review can help a restaurant in the short term, that a bad review is more bark than bite, and that it is the return customer that makes or breaks a restaurant in the long run.

HOW TO USE THIS BOOK

The Boston restaurant scene has changed enormously since I moved to the area in 1977. (Indeed, of the area's 20 best restaurants, 17 were not in existence five years ago—the last time Boston had an up-to-date restaurant guidebook.) This guide is the result of three years of intensive dining in Boston restaurants. During that time, I have visited over 400 restaurants, 95 of which have earned a place in the following pages. I have tried to spare readers my bad experiences, so don't be surprised to find some of the sacred cows of Boston hostelry missing. Each of the restaurants mentioned in this book is in some way remarkable—first and foremost for its food, but sometimes for its striking decor or historic setting.

As a restaurant critic, the two questions I am most frequently asked are: "Where should I go to eat?" and "What is your favorite restaurant?" The first prompts a number of return questions: How much are you willing to spend? What sort of food are you in the mood for? What's the occasion for going out to eat? The second question is harder to answer: there are many restaurants that I like; I don't have a single favorite. L'Espalier is the finest restaurant in Boston, but I would not enjoy dining there more than two or three times a year. I could easily dine weekly at a homey place in my neighborhood called Korea House, but I would be silly to say it was Boston's best. This restaurant guidebook was written to answer both questions, and I hope it will both pique and assuage your hunger in the process.

This guidebook is divided into three sections, the first of which contains critical reviews of over 90 restaurants in Greater Boston. Each review is preceded by practical information about the restaurant: its type of cuisine, its price range, its location, hours, reservation policy, payment and liquor policies, its wheelchair access, special attractions (e.g. entertainment), and dress code. (Note: "major credit cards accepted" refers to Visa and Mastercard—when in doubt, call.) Within the review itself you will find a description of setting, service, and house specialties. Many of the better restaurants offer daily changing menus, so the dishes described are representative of the chef's handiwork rather than items that appear permanently on the bill of fare.

Within this first section, restaurants are grouped into three price ranges: expensive, mid-priced, and cheap. By an expensive restaurant, I mean a place where a full dinner with drinks or a *modest* bottle of wine will cost more than $26 per person; by mid-priced, the same meal will cost $12–26; and by cheap, the same meal will cost less than $12. Within each price range, restaurants are listed in alphabetical order. These categories are at best a crude approximation: remember that lunch costs less than dinner, that chicken costs less than steak. Not everyone orders drinks or wine with dinner. To help you better gauge the cost of a meal at a particular restaurant, I have also listed the price range of the appetizers and entrées. (A rough way to arrive at the total cost is to double that of the entrée.) **Warning:** The prices quoted below hold for summer, 1983. Call the restaurant for an update, or inflate the prices accordingly.

About the Rating System: Following the lead of the Michelin tire company (publishers of the redoubtable French *Guide Michelin*), it has become the practice of American restaurant critics to rate restaurants on a basis of one to four stars, four being the best. Ratings of this sort are useful in that they allow the grouping of restaurants into broad classes of relative quality and value. The limitation of the star system is that it fails to account for single dishes of particular brilliance, or idiosyncrasies of service or setting. Below are definitions of the rating system used in this book.

★★★★ Truly (and consistently) exceptional in all aspects of the food, setting and service. A restaurant must have been in existence for at least three years to qualify for this rating. (Note: Restaurants in this class would be equivalent to a two Michelin star restaurant in France. At this writing, no restaurant in Boston would rate three Michelin stars (the highest).

★★★ Very good (often excellent) food, setting, and service. (Restaurants in this class would rate one star in the Michelin system.)

★★ Above average, with some aspects of the food, setting and service worth a special detour.

★ Average, but with some noteworthy dishes.

Mediocre and bad restaurants have not been included in these pages.

Part II: The second section of this book is designed to help you pick the right restaurant for any occasion, whatever your mood or hunger. Here you will find an extensive cross-reference that indexes the restaurants by cuisine, setting, location, etc.

Part III: The third and final section of this book is even more opinionated than what preceded it. Here you will find a guide to restaurant etiquette, addressing such thorny issues as what to do if you don't like your table, how to send food back, and what constitutes a reasonable tip. You will also find strategies for keeping the price down at any restaurant, be it inexpensive or fancy. Finally, The Critic's Choice—which lists my personal favorites in Boston, the restaurants to which I go when dining out for pleasure.

A CAVEAT

"I am only as good as my last meal," says Boston's most successful restaurateur, Anthony "Pier Four" Athanas. The same should be said for restaurant critics: their pronouncements are only as accurate as the most recent meal they have eaten. The reviews in this book have been based on an average of four meals at each restaurant, and every attempt has been made to revisit each restaurant within six months of the completion of the manuscript.

This notwithstanding, let me say that *at any given time this book will be no more than 90% accurate.* Menus change, prices change, and chefs migrate from restaurant to restaurant like the songbirds with the seasons. There are over 1000 eating establishments in the greater Boston area. Undoubtedly, I have missed some in my listing. Every effort has been made to include only restaurants with proven track records in this book, but it is possible, indeed probable (unfortunately), that one or two entries will no longer belong in this book by the time it is published. No two people have the same taste, and I freely admit that I relish the unusual and the exotic. Please send me your comments, as well as the names of your favorite restaurants (write the Steven Raichlen Cooking School, 7 Temple St., Cambridge, MA 02139) for possible publication in future editions.

One final word—an observation of the great 19th century French chef Antoine Careme. "My chef," complained his employer, the Prince Regent of England, "dinner last night was superb, but you will surely make me die of indigestion." To which the chef replied: "My duty, Sir, is to tempt your appetite, not control it!"

I herewith wish you delectable dining in Boston.

Steven Raichlen
June 9, 1983

"The discovery of a new dish does more for human happiness than the discovery of a new star."
Brillat-Savarin from *Le Physiology du Goût*

I

THE RESTAURANTS

SHOOT THE MOON

Boston's Best Expensive Restaurants

ALLEGRO

Rating: ★★★½

Type of cuisine: Northern Italian

Price range: appetizers from $4.00–7.00; entrees from $14.00–17.00

458 Moody St., Waltham

Telephone: 891–5486

Hours: open for dinner Tuesday–Saturday from 6–9:30 p.m.

Reservations recommended

Major credit cards accepted

Full bar

Wheelchair access adequate

Dress: jacket and tie or turtleneck

The best Italian restaurant in Greater Boston is located in Waltham, not Boston's Italian district in the North End. Its owner is a CIA (Culinary Institute of America)-schooled chef who used to run the popular Harvest restaurant in Cambridge and he does not pretend to be Italian by birth or professional training. When Jim Burke and his partner, Bonita Goodson, purchased the two-year-old Allegro restaurant in 1981, they took on the dual challenge of mastering a cuisine of subtle sophistication in a city where most restaurant goers equate fine Italian cooking with vast portions of spaghetti and meatballs awash with tomato sauce. To judge from the wide critical acclaim, not to mention the overflow crowds of dinner guests, their efforts have been a success.

Allegro was originally opened by a pair of Madeleine Kamman-trained chefs, who chose for the site of their restaurant a seedy neighborhood bar in downtown Waltham. The new owners have left the dining room as it was: a box-like storefront lined with high tech lights, exposed brick walls decorated with Italian travel posters, and Breuer chairs for 50. The high ceilings help diminish the noise (which can be pretty considerable on the weekends) as does the handsome, cubbyhole-like wine rack at the rear of the room. The wait staff sports a new wave look and, considering the sophistication of the food they are serving, is refreshingly down-to-earth.

The Northern Italian food in which Allegro specializes has much in common with French *nouvelle cuisine* with its starchless sauces and sensibly sized portions. But while the French dazzle their guests with exotic ingredients and striking plate presentations, the food at Allegro beguiles the senses with the deceptive simplicity of its flavors. A first course might consist of a salad of veal ravioli or homemade angel's hair spaghetti that manages to be feather-light while at the same time delectably chewy. (*Note*: pasta is served only as a first course here but the restaurant does sell its excellent homemade noodles in gourmet shops around the city.) Entrees might include grilled salmon with lobster sausage or a grilled pheasant served with *pancetta* (Italian bacon) and shallots, which stands out in my mind as the only pheasant I have tasted in Boston that wasn't dry. On a recent visit, a side dish of vegetables featured a miniature eggplant while desserts ranged from chocolate orange torte to homemade praline ice cream.

The much deserved popularity of Allegro has led to its major drawback. There is no lounge or waiting area for people who arrive before their table is ready. For their part, guests of the first seating have complained of being asked to leave the restaurant before they are ready. A complimentary cocktail or glass of wine from the excellent Italian wine list would be appreciated when such circumstances arise.

ANOTHER SEASON

Rating: ★★★

Type of cuisine: contemporary/Continental

Price range: appetizers from $3.50–4.25; entrees from $9.00–16.00

97 Mt. Vernon St., Boston

Telephone: 367–0880

Hours: open for lunch Tuesday–Friday from 12–2 p.m.; for dinner Monday–Saturday from 6–10 p.m.

Reservations recommended

Major credit cards accepted

Wine and beer

Wheelchair access difficult

Dress: jacket and tie or turtleneck

Don't complain to Another Season owner, Odette Bery, about the infelicities of English cooking. For the past 20 years the London-born chef has endeavored to improve the culinary reputation of her country-men. Bery has opened three popular Boston restaurants: the late Orson Welles Restaurant, the Turtle Cafe, and, in 1977, her crowning achievement, Another Season.

The name of Bery's restaurant tells only part of the story—her commitment to serving seasonal seafood and produce Although she trained at the arch-traditional Cordon Bleu of London, Bery's cooking today is strongly influenced by Mexican, Indian, and Oriental recipes and, above all, by French *nouvelle cuisine.*

Bery's bimonthly menu features such specialties as fettucini with smoked trout, beef tenderloin *bruxelloise* (with braised vegetables), and chicken *el pipan* served with a haunting sauce of green tomatoes and pumpkin seeds. Her cold dishes, like *ceviche* (marinated, uncooked scallops) and duck salad Gascony are mercifully free of the sort of caloric overkill that mars so many restaurant appetizers. Desserts include a white chocolate almond cake and silk-smooth chocolate regal. The wine list harbors lots of half bottles and drinking values as well as pricier vintages.

Few restaurants are more romantic than this Beacon Hill basement with its charming murals of top-hatted gentlemen and bejeweled ladies of

Gay Nineties Paris. For added intimacy, the dining area has been divided into several small rooms separated by French doors. For all this, Bery denies that she is after the "heavy bucks" and perhaps the best thing about her restaurant is the surprisingly reasonable prices.

APLEY'S

Rating: ★★★★

Type of cuisine: contemporary

Price range: appetizers from $4.00–8.00; entrees from $16.00–25.00

39 Dalton Street, the Sheraton-Boston Hotel, Boston

Telephone: 236–2000

Hours: open for dinner seven nights a week with seatings at 6, 7 and 8 p.m.

Reservations recommended

Major credit cards accepted

Full bar

Wheelchair access fair

Dress: suit or jacket and tie

Apley's opened at the downtown Sheraton in November, 1981, with a fanfare worthy of the new signature restaurant of the international Sheraton Corporation. The dining room received a million-dollar facelift and the kitchen acquired a hydroponic herb garden and live trout tank. The chef had carte blanche to fly in fresh truffles and foie gras from France and the waiters were even trained at video-taped practice sessions!

The master mind behind the extravagance was a mercurial chef named Robert Brody, whose visions set a new standard for hotel dining in Boston. Brody began with dishes exemplifying *nouvelle cuisine*, the "new" French cooking, and then applied Gallic cooking techniques to indigenous foods of New England: Cohasset mussels, New Hampshire trout and Nantucket pheasant. His experiments culminated in an unseemly New England cassoulet, an haute culinary reinterpretation of the Boston classic, baked beans.

Brody left Apley's in January, 1983, but his successor, English-born David Woodward, has ably picked up the torch. New house specialties include salmon with mustard sauce, pheasant with pecan soubise (onion pureé), veal with Stilton sauce, and ginger sherbet with home candied fruit. Woodward has retained the unique "Apley's premier," a fixed price main course that enables guests to sample small portions of two different entrees on a single plate.

Apley's service remains fanatic in its attention to detail: water glasses are filled with sparkling Saratoga Springs water, the butter comes in rosette-shaped pats, and toasted bagel slices (a house bread specialty) ride on fiercely starched, intricately folded napkins. The wine list boasts a number of premium French and Californian vintages; Grand Marnier "Centenaire" (made with 100-year-old brandy) and Hennessy "Paradis" (extremely old cognac) are available for post-prandial sipping.

Depending on your outlook, the sleek grey and silver decor complete with chrome armchairs, plush sofas, and a split-level, glass-lined dining area, will seem boldly contemporary or a little chilly. A harpist or classical guitarist provides the pleasure of live dinner music.

BAY TOWER ROOM

Rating: ★★

Type of cuisine: Continental

Price range: appetizers from $3.00–10.00; entrees from $15.00–20.00

60 State Street, Boston

Telephone: 723–1666

Hours: open for dinner Monday–Saturday from 5:30–10:00 p.m.

Reservations recommended

Major credit cards accepted

Full bar

Wheelchair access fair

Entertainment: dancing nightly

Dress: suit or jacket and tie

I am always amazed at how the right ambiance can improve a lackluster dinner—a case in point is the Bay Tower Room located on the 33rd floor of a downtown skyscraper. The drinks can be warm, the service slow, and the Continental cuisine adequate but in no way remarkable. It just tastes that way, seasoned as it is by a breathtaking view that embraces Quincy Market, Boston Harbor, Logan Airport and the Customs House clock tower (the latter close enough to almost touch).

The Bay Tower Room is at its best with simple dishes: fresh oysters, attractively garnished caviar and smoked salmon, Caesar salad, roast rack of lamb, or chateaubriand expertly carved at your tableside. The problems begin with the fancier fare: seafood drowned in heavy sauces or lobster entombed in soggy puff pastry. Fortunately, the house desserts make up for previous shortcomings, including a towering iced Grand Marnier soufflé, a Kahlua-laced chocolate mousse, and a baked Alaska that would be even better served slightly warm.

The dining area is divided into many little tiers and alcoves to foster a feeling of intimacy. The bustle from the lounge on the balcony fills the place with excitement. The well-spaced tables boast the amenities of heavy silver, gold-rimmed china and lamplight. The busboys wear white jackets with gold epaulettes but, considering the steep price of dinner, the service can be slow.

After dinner, you can ascend to a postage-stamp-sized dance floor to whirl beneath the stars to the strains of the Larry Smith Orchestra. No matter what the quality of your dinner, you will leave this romantic spot enchanted.

BLUE STRAWBERY

Rating: ★★★

Type of cuisine: contemporary

Price range: Pris-fixe dinner for $25.00

29 Ceres St., Portsmouth, New Hampshire

Telephone: (603) 431–6420

Hours: Dinner served Monday–Saturday with seatings at 6 and 9 p.m., Sunday with seatings at 3 and 6 p.m.

No credit cards, but personal checks accepted

Full bar

Wheelchair access good

Dress: jacket and tie or turtleneck

Way back before anybody had ever heard of kiwi fruits or green pepper-corns and before Paul Bocuse landed on the cover of *Newsweek*, a chef in Portsmouth, New Hampshire, was specializing in *nouvelle cuisine.* Since 1971 James Haller has blithely disregarded culinary convention (not to mention recipes) and dreamed up wild flavor combinations that taste as good as their names sound outlandish. For the site of the restaurant Haller and partners chose an old ship's chandlery in a derelict waterfront warehouse. The name of the place was as whimsical as the menu: the restaurant was called the Blue Strawbery.

Countless restaurants have opened in restored warehouses since then, of course, and among contemporary chefs, new ingredient combinations have become as old hat as boiled dinners. But chef Haller continues to cook to a different drummer and, as a result, the Blue Strawbery still delights both novice and seasoned restaurant-goers.

The Blue Strawbery offers seatings at 6 p.m. and 9 p.m. and guests take their places at mismatched tables set with silver and Wedgwood china, no two pieces of which are alike. Nor is there a printed menu. Dinner is a fixed price, five course feast that changes daily. Everyone receives the same appetizer, salad, and dessert, and a choice from among two or three first courses and entrees. Most of the food is served family-style with seconds to be had for the asking.

Dinner usually begins with soup—a rich cream of mushroom with sherry or perhaps a corn and pumpkin chowder—served in a coffee mug that might have come from a YMCA cafeteria. First courses range from frogs legs with mustard hollandaise to smoked salmon in frozen papaya custard. A sherbet or salad comes next, the latter tossed with a weird but wonderful brown sugar dressing. The main course could include beef tournedos with goose liver sauce, roast duckling with Portuguese sausage and oranges, or swordfish topped with crabmeat and amaretto. The only dish that does not vary is dessert: fresh strawberries with brown sugar and sour cream for dipping.

A small upstairs dining area has been added to the main dining room with its time-stained brick walls decorated with paintings of 19th century ships and sea captains. The service is courteous, the drinks are strong, but the frequently changing wine list, at least on our last visit, did not measure up to the food. Another small criticism: each dish is so elaborate and flavorful, one would welcome some simply prepared starches or vegetables.

CAFE BUDAPEST

Rating: ★★★

Type of cuisine: Hungarian/Central European

Price range: appetizers from $2.50–7.00; entrees from $10.00–18.00

90 Exeter St., Boston

Telephone: 734-3388

Hours: open for lunch Monday–Saturday from 12–3 p.m.; for dinner Sunday–Thursday from 5–10:30 p.m.; Sunday from 1–10:30 p.m.

Reservations recommended

Major credit cards accepted

Full bar

Wheelchair access poor

Dress: suit

"If music be the food of love, play on," sighed Shakespeare's Orsino. Edith Ban has made the bard's admonition house policy at the renowned Café Budapest. Nightly music played by a violin-piano duet in a lounge accoutered with private alcoves, flocked wallpaper, and marble topped tables is only part of what makes the restaurant so uniquely romantic.

Born in Hungary, the white-garbed Ban runs her restaurant like a personal fiefdom, preparing many of the sauces herself and keeping the recipes secret even from her employees. Ban's fanaticism has a happy conclusion in such Café Budapest specialties as chicken *paprikas* with homemade egg noodles, *wienerschnitzel* à la Holstein, and a *sauerbraten* with a cranberry-cinnamon sauce so succulent, a mouthful will leave you speechless. The house soups, like Hungarian country-style soup with chicken liver dumpling and the exquisite iced tart cherry soup, manage to be simultaneously robust and delicate. Such homemade Viennese pastries as champagne torte and multi-layer Dobos torte are in high demand but, whenever I dine at the Café Budapest, I order the feather-light cherry strudel. Don't bother trying to pronounce the names on the wine list but such vintages as *Badacsony Szurkebarat* (a full-bodied white) and *Tokaji Aszu* (a luscious dessert wine) serve to remind us that reasonably priced, fine wines have been made in Hungary since Roman times.

Located in the basement of the Copley Square Hotel, the Café Budapest has three dining rooms plus a lounge. I prefer the gingerbread-house-like *Weinstube* with its leaded glass windows and hand-painted ceiling beams to the richly paneled but impersonal main dining room and the pink room with its tables graced with fresh roses. Don't miss the complimentary liver pâté (you can taste the chicken fat) in the lounge. The service can range from solicitous to supercilious. Dinner is better than lunch.

THE CAFE PLAZA

Rating: ★★★

Type of cuisine: Continental/breakfast

Price range: breakfast fare $5.75–6.50; dinner expensive

Copley Plaza Hotel, Copley Square, Boston

Telephone: 267–5300

Hours: open for breakfast Monday–Saturday from 7–10 a.m.; Sunday from 8 a.m.–noon; for lunch Monday–Friday from 12–2 p.m.; and for dinner Monday–Saturday from 5:30–10:30 p.m.

Reservations recommended

Major credit cards accepted

Full bar

Wheelchair access good

Piano music nightly in the Plaza bar and the main dining room

Dress: jacket and tie required

The Grande Dame of Boston hostelry will probably be mortified to learn that she has just been named the best breakfast spot in Boston. After all, the Copley Plaza, once the sister hotel of the prestigious Park Plaza in New York (the double P emblem is still well in evidence), boasts no fewer than seven drinking and dining environments. To single out the Café Plaza for breakfast would be to risk overlooking brunch in the Victoriana-filled Copley's Restaurant, halfshell fare in the high ceilinged, brass and fern-lined Copley Bar, high tea complete with watercress sandwiches at the Palm Court in the lobby, and drinks (try the "ice blue" martini) in the ornate Plaza Bar.

True, the Café Plaza is the pride of the Grande Dame but why mention this formal dining room—with its morning-coated maitre d', encyclopedic wine list, and tinkling baby grand—in the context of so trivial a meal as breakfast? The truth is that the Café Plaza breakfast is as good a morning meal as you'll find anywhere and, for a price infinitely more affordable than that of dinner, you can enjoy one of the most splendid dining rooms in town.

Where else are corned beef hash and eggs Benedict served by squadrons of epauletted busboys beneath Waterford chandeliers, gleaming mahogany, and a soaring, barrel-vaulted ceiling remarkable for the intricacy of its stucco? Where else do goblets of freshly squeezed juice arrive on paper doilies? Where do croissants and billowy pumpkin spice muffins come with miniature jars of imported Tiptree marmalade? And where are omelettes filled with apples and boursin cheese? Given the magnificence of the vast swag curtains, the marble floors, and Oriental vases, who cares that the bangor sausages are unappealingly starchy?

There are worse fates than dinner at the Café Plaza where house specialties range from asparagus wrapped in *gravad lax* (Swedish salt and dill-cured salmon) and oysters Kirkpatrick (topped with cheese and bacon), to blood-rare duck "steak" with cherries and lobster brunetiére with oysters. (A newly-instituted "taster's menu" enables parties of two, four, or even larger numbers to sample these and other items in a seven-course banquet.) It's just that dinner at the Copley Plaza is just another high-priced hotel meal whereas breakfast here is truly an experience fit for a king.

CHILLINGSWORTH

Rating: ★★★★

Type of cuisine: French

Price range: complete dinners from $25.50–37.50

Route 6A, Brewster

Telephone: 896–3640

Hours: Chillingsworth is open on the weekend from mid-May to mid-June and from September to the end of October; open Tuesday–Sunday from Memorial Day to Labor Day. Seatings for dinner are at 6–6:30 p.m. and at 9–9:30 p.m.; from July 4 to Labor Day, Sunday brunch from 11:30 a.m.–2 p.m.

Reservations required

Major credit cards accepted

Full bar

Wheelchair access good

Dress: jacket and tie

Robert Rabin may be the only chef in New England to have been invited to teach the French how to cook. In April, 1983, the 35-year-old Cape Cod restaurateur demonstrated the preparation of clam chowder, cheesecake, and other American specialties to a prestigious gastronomic society in Lyons. Rabin and his wife, Pat, run an extraordinary French restaurant in Brewster called Chillingsworth and their training with some of the top chefs in Paris, not to mention their willingness to work 100-hour weeks for the duration of the tourist season, has enabled the young couple to provide a dining experience less reminiscent of a typical Cape Cod restaurant than of a Michelin-starred dining establishment in France.

Chillingsworth may be located in a three-century-old mansion but the Rabins are decidedly contemporary in their cooking and in their taste. Their *pris-fixe* dinner includes hors d'oeuvres, an appetizer, soup, salad, mid-meal sherbet, entree, and dessert with petits fours. The family garden supplies the kitchen with fresh herbs and vegetables for the daily changing menu. Appetizers might include a lobster mousse or *boudin blanc* (homemade veal sausage) served with quickly sautéed wild mushrooms. Entrees could range from a grilled, marjoram-scented breast of pheasant to rack of lamb with fresh coriander leaf to an ingenious "three salmon" plate shared by salmon sashimi, smoked salmon with cream sauce, and moist, poached salmon with herbs. The chilled plum soup, invented by Pat Rabin, is a masterpiece and the cold melon soup was featured in *Gourmet Magazine*. Pat also runs the pastry kitchen, preparing such delicacies as tarragon sherbet, hot peach soufflé, and a wanton "velours of chocolate" made with chocolate mousse and sponge cake. As in any fine restaurant in France, a plate of *mignardises* (tiny cookies) is served with coffee and homemade chocolate truffles accompany the check.

Named for the son of its first owner, Chillingsworth was built in 1689. One of its dining rooms retains the original, hand-painted Zuber wallpaper (its twin hangs in the White House in Washington). To foster intimacy, the dining area has been divided among five ground floor rooms which are filled with 18th century furniture and antique import china. On a more contemporary note, the lounge is set in a greenhouse and hors d'oeuvres and desserts can be enjoyed at tables in the garden.

THE HARVEST RESTAURANT

Rating: ★★★½

Type of cuisine: contemporary

Price range: café menu appetizers $2.50–6.00; entrees $7.00–13.00; dining room menu appetizers $4.00–8.00, entrees $15.00–21.00

44 Brattle Street, Cambridge

Telephone: 492–1115

Hours: open for lunch Monday–Saturday from 11:30–2:30 p.m; for dinner Sunday–Friday from 6–10 p.m., Saturday till 10:30 p.m.; Sunday brunch from noon–3 p.m.

Reservations recommended for the dining room; not accepted for the café or the terrace

Major credit cards accepted

Full bar

Wheelchair access good

Dress: jacket and tie in the dining room; nice casual in the café

Since it opened in 1975, the Harvest Restaurant has regularly received *Boston Magazine*'s "Best of Boston" award for its lively singles bar, Ben's Corner. But to come here for the social scene alone would be to miss out on a shady terrace, a bustling café (whose burgers are reputed to be the best in Cambridge), and a formal dining room run by a chef who made the Honor Roll of American chefs in *Food and Wine* magazine. Many people find the Harvest expensive, trendy, and, in a strangely casual way, pretentious (self-conscious might be a better word). Since its founding, however, this Harvard Square restaurant complex has been a citywide trend-setter, pioneering homemade pasta, regional American cooking, wild game, and even "trash fish" (under-utilized sea creatures such as monkfish, wolf fish, and shark) long before these foods became popular at other contemporary establishments.

Innovation has forever been the battle cry of the Harvest kitchen which has trained some of the top chefs in Boston, like Jim Burke of Allegro. The current chef, Cape Cod-born Robert Kinkead, applies the starchless reduction sauces and offbeat seasonings of French *nouvelle cuisine* to the robust flavors of the Mediterranean, Latin America, and even our own Deep South. Among his most recent creations are a smoked shrimp Bavarian, roasted vegetable and chilled lamb salad, beef with shallot soufflé, wolf fish with red pepper butter, and grilled pork loin served with six different kinds of Mexican chilis. Desserts will delight the chocoholic, ranging from a moist midnight chocolate cake to white chocolate mousse cake to a chocolate marquise that's as rich and smooth as its main ingredient, butter. Ice creams and sherbets are made on the premises as are the three kinds of bread found in the bread basket. At this writing, plans are underway to install a barbecue grill on the terrace where fish, meat, and game will be grilled over mesquite wood and grape-vine fires.

Meals in the café and main dining room differ in their presentation and prices but not in their originality. The menu changes daily (its cover was designed by Milton Glazer). What does not change is the excellent French bread (not the crusty kind but chewy like a bagel) and the homemade chocolate truffles that accompany the check in the dining room.

Founded by Ben and Jane Thompson (renovators of Faneuil Hall), the Harvest boasts a typical Cantabridgian setting of seasonally changing Marimekko wall fabrics (the Thompsons introduced Marimekko to the United States), Breuer chairs, and sturdy stoneware instead of delicate china. The popular Harvest Café has butcher block tables, colorful cushions, and a window with a view into the kitchen. The terrace, shaded with beach umbrellas and box trees strung with Christmas tree lights, makes an idyllic spot for drinks, dessert, or a light lunch or supper. Service in the main dining room can be a bit more casual than you would expect when you are paying upwards of $80.00 for two for dinner.

ICARUS

Rating: ★★★

Type of cuisine: contemporary

Price range: appetizers from $4.50–6.00; entrees from $13.00–19.00

540 Tremont St., Boston

Telephone: 426–1790

Hours: open for dinner Tuesday–Thursday from 6–10 p.m., Friday and Saturday, till 11:30; Sunday brunch from 11–3

Reservations recommended

Major credit cards accepted

Beer and wine

Wheelchair access difficult

Dress: Nice casual to jacket and tie

The Icarus of Greek mythology was an incorrigibly curious youth who strapped on wax wings, flew to the sun, and perished as a result of his own curiosity when the sun's rays melted his wings. Hardly a consoling image for chefs who, perforce, spend their days in a sweltering kitchen. But Tom Hall and John Bellot, owners of this attractive South End restaurant, have managed to skirt the perils of blazing broilers and scalding stockpots and, in the process, have transformed a pleasant neighborhood eatery into a restaurant of considerable distinction.

Gone is the blackboard where the bill of fare was written by hand, and in its stead is a handsome, printed menu which changes daily and proposes such innovations as roquefort mousse, cream of red pepper soup, and brook trout with kumquat sauce. True to French *nouvelle cuisine,* the sauces are made without starchy thickeners and are built on lengthily simmered stocks, flavored with fresh herbs (and, occasionally, too much salt). House specialties include rack of lamb and chicken *roulade* (boned, stuffed, and rolled chicken) each served with a nightly changing sauce. A Northern Italian influence can be seen in such Icarus offerings as hand-rolled linguine with hazelnuts and *pancetta* (Italian bacon) and angel's hair spaghetti with wild mushrooms and sweetbreads.

The vegetables here, cooked and served *al dente*, retain all their garden freshness. The pleasure of the chocolate gâteau, a long-time house specialty made without an ounce of flour, lingers long after the waiter has cleared your plate. Coffee at Icarus is a major production: a coffee filter with fresh grounds and pot of boiling water are brought to the table and you are even provided with whole cinnamon sticks for dipping in your coffee. The resulting beverage, while admirably fresh, would probably be warmer if prepared in the kitchen. The wine list is laudable in its scope but could use a few more modestly priced bottles.

Just over a year ago, Icarus was remodeled, making way for a separate entryway (faced with stunning art nouveau stained glass) and a small auxiliary dining room. The main dining room has the eclectic charm of antique mantelpieces, turn-of-the-century lamps, mission oak tables and chairs, no two of which match any more than the plates and antique silverware that adorn them. Overhead stands a sculpture of Icarus posed for flight and indolently whirling paddle fans. Icarus makes an attractive Sunday brunch spot, its specialties ranging from the usual eggs Benedict to ham *pithiviers* (puff pastry cake) and French toast with strawberries and honey-cinnamon butter. The service is well-mannered but leisurely.

JULIEN (at the HOTEL MERIDIEN)

Rating: ★★★½

Type of cuisine: French/*nouvelle cuisine*

Price range: appetizers $7.00–13.00; entrees from $18.00–26.00; fixed price sit-down brunch in the Julien $19.00 (holidays, $24.00)

250 Franklin Street, Boston

Telephone: 451–1900

Hours: open for lunch Monday–Friday from noon–2 p.m.; for dinner Sunday–Thursday from 6–9:30 p.m., Friday and Saturday 6–10 p.m.; Sunday brunch seatings at 11:30 a.m. and 1:30 p.m.

Reservations recommended

Major credit cards accepted

Full bar

Wheelchair access fair

Entertainment: piano music 7 nights a week

Dress: jacket and tie

It's a good thing that restaurant critics return to the scene of the crime. Two years ago I reviewed the Julien Restaurant at the then newly opened Hotel Meridien, reporting that the high priced fare looked as though it was prepared by a kitchen brigade of linebackers. On a recent visit here, I enjoyed one of the best meals I have ever had in Boston.

Named for Boston's first French restaurant (opened by one Jean-Baptiste Julien in 1794), the Julien is the formal dining room of the Hotel Meridien (run by Air France) which opened in Post Office Square in November, 1981. The location—the old Federal Reserve Building (built in 1922 and modeled on a Renaissance Palace in Rome)—is historic but the food is not. The menu boasts the latest innovations of French *nouvelle cuisine* conceived by Gerard Vié, a Meridien consultant whose Trois Marches restaurant in Versailles has two coveted Michelin stars. Actually, much of the credit for the Julien's extraordinary menu goes to Michel Pepin, the 27-year-old chef from Beaujolais, whose boyish figure is dwarfed by his towering toque.

Dinner at the Meridien begins with a complimentary hors d'oeuvre —a checkerboard of smoked fish and chives, for example, or a pair of mussels topped with tarragon-scented tomato sauce. Appetizers range from Vié's *salade à ma façon* (duck liver, scallop, and crayfish salad) to a *terrine de celeri nouveau au foie de canard* (duck liver and celery pâté served on an unusual lettuce mousse, the pâté an extraordinary approximation of buttery French *foie gras*). Entrees include *canard au vinaigre de cidre et au miel* (duckling with cider vinegar and honey, the breast served rare on one plate, the thigh in a salad on another) and *ragoût de petoncles et ris de veau* (sweetbreads, scallops, wild mushrooms and pasta). But the pièce de resistance is the *raviolis de homard aux truffes* (lobster ravioli with truffles). Imagine a lobster stunningly reconstructed from the head and tail of the shellfish, the body made from lobster stew and lobster-filled ravioli, the "legs" ingeniously formed from green beans and tiny eggplants, and you'll understand my admiration for Meridien chef Pepin.

The cheese platter does not live up to the rest of the meal but the three tiered pastry cart makes up for it, loaded with such delicacies as a raspberry-almond tile Napoleon and a chocolate mousse cake that redefines the meaning of the word "decadent." Coffee is served with the fanfare of a four sugar entourage but the lack of fresh decaffeinated coffee is an egregious shortcoming. *Mignardises* (tiny cakes and cookies served with dessert) help sweeten the formidable moment of reckoning. The wine list prices make usury seem cheap but we did find one bargain in the form of a 1981 pinot chardonnay from Enofriulia, remarkable in its effervescent finesse.

Located in the former Members Court of the old Federal Reserve Building, the Julien boasts the elegance of lofty ceilings, gilded cornices, and stone walls faced with manicured espalier. Guests sit in wingback Queen Anne chairs at tables set with heavy silver, imported china, lamplight, and Peruvian lilies. Background music is supplied by the piano in the elegant Julien Lounge. (Be sure to admire the paintings here by N. C. Wyeth.) The black tie service is attentive but a wee bit leisurely.

A fixed price brunch is served in the Julien dining room, as is a wheeled buffet lunch. The Café Fleuri, the informal dining room, boasts a sumptuous brunch buffet highlighted by butter unicorns and excellent warm croissants.

LENORA

Rating: ★★★

Type of cuisine: contemporary

Price range: appetizers $4.00–5.50; entrees from $12.50–19.00

1812 Mass. Ave., Cambridge

Telephone: 661–0191

Hours: open for lunch Monday–Friday from 11:30–2:30 p.m.; open for dinner Monday–Thursday from 5:30–9:30 p.m., Friday–Saturday till 10 p.m., Sunday from 5–9 p.m.; Sunday brunch from 11:30–3 p.m.

Reservations recommended

Major credit cards accepted

Full bar

Wheelchair access good

Dress: jacket and tie or turtleneck

The pretty Lenora must be one of the best kept restaurant secrets in Cambridge. Who would expect to find first rate *nouvelle* American cooking in a striking, contemporary setting amid the bleak construction of Porter Square? I've long praised the brunch at Lenora, with its classical guitarist and menu offering such Franco-American improvisations as bourbon French toast and poached eggs with hollandaise sauce in a popover. Dinner here may lack the finesse of that of a restaurant like Panache or Upstairs at the Pudding, but that does not prevent most guests from leaving the restaurant enchanted with their evening.

Lenora is named for Lenora Bowen, a former mathematics professor, who, with her husband, weary of academe, purchased a country inn in West Stockbridge. The couple returned to Cambridge to open the restaurant in 1981. (Stuart Bowen mans the front of the restaurant; Lenora runs the kitchen.) Bowen sums up her cooking as "fresh seasonal American ingredients prepared in the French style," an apt description for such creations as butternut squash bisque, swordfish with pecan pesto, and duckling with bourbon lemon sauce. (The thigh meat of the latter is ground into sausage and stuffed into the breast which is served a little well-done for my taste but then, I like my duck breast rare.) The size of the portions is American, too: no *nouvelle cuisine* parsimony of three string beans and a tiny new potato accompanies Lenora's entrees but rather a copious entourage of wild rice, redolent red cabbage, and spinach spruced up with sautéed cherry tomatoes. A large salad topped with crisp bread crumbs comes with the price of an entree; so do admirably plump popovers which are served piping hot from the oven.

You would never guess that this restaurant seats 90, as the dining area is divided between four small rooms, each furnished with track lights, comfortable wood-armed chairs (with an occasional antique), and walls painted in pinks and mauves and blues. Soft lamplight illuminates well-spaced tables graced with flowered fabrics and fresh cut flowers. The stainless steel flatware, however, is unworthy of the handsome gold and red-rimmed plates. The service is friendly, a little awkward, and mercifully unpretentious.

L'ESPALIER

Rating: ★★★★

Type of cuisine: French

Price range: pris-fixe dinners from $37.00

30 Gloucester Street, Boston

Telephone: 262–3023

Hours: open for lunch Monday–Friday from noon–2 p.m.; for dinner
Monday–Friday from 6–10:30 p.m., Saturday 6–10:30 p.m.

Reservations recommended

Major credit cards accepted

Full bar

Wheelchair access poor

Dress: suit or jacket and tie

It isn't easy running the best restaurant in the city. Ask Moncef Meddeb
and Donna Doll, the owners of the prestigious L'Espalier. In a typical
week Moncef works a bone-numbing 80 hours, presiding over 12 cooks
who daily make fresh breads, ice creams and petits fours. Donna runs the
front of the "house" which seats a mere 55 on the first two floors of a 19th
century townhouse that the couple have restored to museum perfection.

L'Espalier opened in 1978 in a second floor Boylston Street storefront where Moncef Meddeb quickly distinguished himself as a chef of
keen sensitivity, tempering the extravagant innovations of *nouvelle
cuisine* with the purity of classical French cooking. The French-born
Tunisian made his sauces from lengthily simmered stocks, enriched with
butter and cream and devoid of starchy thickeners. Small farms around
New England furnished the restaurant with specially raised squab, trout
and produce while importers scoured the French countryside for wild
mushrooms, raw milk cheeses and even Mediterranean fish flown in
from Paris. The fixed price menu changes weekly and features such
delicacies as smoked seafood-citrus salad, squab with garlic-liver sauce,
veal with lobster, and lamb with goat cheese ravioli. The way to experience Moncef's cooking at its best is to order a *menu dégustation* ("tasting
menu") that enables a couple to share successive sets of appetizers and

entrees, transforming the meal into a six-course feast for the eyes and palate.

Seeking a showcase for Moncef's extraordinary food, the couple moved their restaurant in August of 1982 to a Victorian townhouse in the Back Bay. Guests await their tables in a *salon* with a massive fireplace (a popular spot for after-dinner drinks, too) and are seated for dinner in a high-ceilinged parlor with intricate stucco and an ornate marble mantelpiece. A second dining room upstairs, decorated with stuffed game birds and period canvases, has the charm of an English hunting lodge. The service is solicitous, tense, and mannered.

The main drawback to L'Espalier is its formidable expense. Dinner for two with cheese (don't miss the excellent cheese platter) and wine (from a list with an excellent selection of top notch Bordeaux and Burgundies) could run $125–$150. People with large appetites may find the exquisitely arranged portions small.

LOCKE-OBER CAFE

Rating: ★★★½

Type of cuisine: Continental/New England

Price range: appetizers $2.00–13.00; entrees $8.00–20.00

3 Winter Place, Boston

Telephone: 542–1340

Hours: open for lunch Monday–Saturday from 11 a.m.–3 p.m.; for dinner Monday–Saturday from 3–10 p.m., Friday and Saturday till 10:30 p.m.

Reservations recommended

Major credit cards accepted

Full bar

Wheelchair access adequate

Dress: suit or jacket and tie

"A trip to Boston without visiting Locke-Ober's would be like going to Agra and ignoring the Taj Mahal," observed the poet Ogden Nash, a frequent patron of this historic Boston restaurant. Hyperbole, perhaps, but in its own understated way Locke-Ober's *does* offer the quintessential Boston dining experience: timeless Continental fare served by wry, sexagenarian waiters amid the meticulously preserved trappings of a nineteenth century men's club. Boston has changed a lot since Louis Ober opened his elegant Restaurant Parisien on a quiet downtown cul-de-sac, but at his legacy, Locke-Ober's, time has stood still.

The current Locke-Ober's resulted from the improbable union of a boisterous saloon called Frank Locke's Wine Room with the neighboring fancy French restaurant run by Louis Ober. (The key to the portal joining the restaurants was ceremoniously pitched into the harbor in 1897.) The dual nature of the restaurant's origin is still apparent in its extensive menu which proposes such Continental classics as *petite marmite* (vegetable and beef-loaded consommé) and sweetbreads *financière* alongside such hardy New England dishes as oyster stew, finnan haddie, and the best Indian pudding in town. Let upstart chefs cook with raspberry vinegar and green peppercorns; in this age of rampant *nouvelle cuisine*, it is refreshing to receive huge portions of unabashedly rich food awash in cream sauce.

House specialties at the venerable Locke-Ober's include oysters à la Gino (topped with crumbs and bacon), chicken Richmond (served with fresh mushrooms and Smithfield ham under a bell jar), and delectable steak tartare. True, the Caesar salad is oily and it's a shame to muck up perfectly good shellfish with tomato sauce in the overrated lobster Savannah, but the sultana roll with claret sauce and devastatingly rich English trifle serve to ensure that customers will leave the restaurant with smiles upon their faces.

Locke-Ober's historic setting alone is worth the steep price of admission. Although the service is marginally more gracious upstairs, newcomers do well to dine in the ground floor Men's Bar (open to women since 1968) decorated with gilded wall paper, a hand-carved Dominican mahogany bar, and a portrait of the rosy, nude Mlle. Yvette which is draped in black whenever Harvard loses the game to Yale. The elegant Ober Room upstairs has been meticulously restored with mahogany paneling, gilded mantelpieces, and glass-doored china cabinets from a Newburyport mansion. The private dining rooms on the third floor are popular with local businessmen.

MAISON ROBERT

Rating: ★★

Type of cuisine: French

Price range: for Bonhomme Richard (the formal dining room): appetizers $4.25–16.00, entrees $15.00–23.00

Price range: for Ben's Café (the informal dining room downstairs): appetizers $2.50–9.25; entrees $9.00–19.00

45 School St., Boston

Telephone: 227–3370

Hours: open for lunch Monday–Friday from 11–2:30 p.m.; for dinner Sunday–Friday from 5:30–9 p.m.; Saturday till 10:30 p.m.

Reservations recommended

Major credit cards accepted

Full bar

Wheelchair access adequate

Dress: suit or jacket and tie (less formal downstairs)

This is the house that Robert built. It is located in Boston's Old City Hall building, worth a visit in itself for the purity of its Second Empire architecture. The formal dining room, Bonhomme Richard ("Poor Richard," a reference to the statue of Benjamin Franklin in the courtyard), has high ceilings, gleaming chandeliers, and rust-colored curtains framing a serene view of the Granary Burial Ground. A less formal restaurant occupies the basement of Robert's house: Ben's Cafe, faced with softly lit brick walls and barrel vaulted ceiling of what was formerly the city vault. There is even an outdoor terrace lined with umbrellaed tables, a lunchtime oasis amid the bustle of downtown.

The Robert of Maison Robert is Lucien Robert, a Normandy-born chef who trained with the legendary Prunier of Paris before moving to the United States and meeting his wife and partner, Ann, in Madison, Wisconsin. Since moving to Boston, the couple has had three restaurants; Maison Robert, the most recent, opened at Old City Hall in 1972. Although schooled in classical French cuisine, Lucien Robert has kept pace with the present by proposing such innovations as terrine of leeks and warm oysters with artichokes in puff pastry alongside such traditional items as veal Orloff, brains with brown butter, and calf's liver with bacon and marrow. Back before anyone had ever heard of monkfish, Lucien Robert flew fresh *lotte* in from France to be served with saffron and mussels. And unique to this restaurant is a visiting chefs' program that regularly brings one- and two-star chefs from France to prepare their specialties at Maison Robert.

All is not flawless at this elegant restaurant, however, particularly at Ben's Café. Among the more striking infelicities are salty appetizers, miserly cheese trays, and sauces that would make epoxy glue seem light. *Tarte tatin* (upside-down apple pie) is the house dessert specialty: when it is hot, it is very, very good, when it is cold, it's like shoe leather.

Maison Robert is not an inexpensive restaurant, but, upstairs at least, you do get your money's worth from the service. The captains, fluent in French and German as well as English, have a graciousness and professionalism just not found at boutique restaurants. Stunning photographs of Maison Robert's wine cellar illustrate the extensive, expensive wine list. At the budget end of the listing, the Métaire muscadet, which the restaurant imports directly, is particularly recommended.

Service downstairs can be problematic, however. Popular with area businessmen, Maison Robert has private dining rooms for small to middle-sized parties.

MILL FALLS

Rating: ★★

Type of cuisine: Continental

Price range: appetizers $2.50–5.00; entrees from $13.00–19.00 (less expensive at lunch)

383 Elliot St., Newton Upper Falls

Telephone: 244–3080

Hours: open for lunch Monday–Friday from 11:45 a.m.–2:30 p.m.; for dinner Monday–Saturday from 5:30–11 p.m.

Reservations recommended

Major credit cards accepted

Full bar

Wheelchair access adequate

Entertainment: nightly at the piano bar in the lounge

Dress: jacket and tie

On this spot, so the legend goes, the Indian Chief Nahanton pledged the hand of his only daughter. It would be hard to pick a more scenic site for a restaurant than the historic Mill Falls on the Charles River, facing a centenarian span known as Echo Bridge. Once a grist mill and then a silk factory, today the Mill Falls is a restaurant, serving solid Continental fare that appeals to its lunchtime business crowd. The lounge with its piano bar, the dining room with its well-spaced tables set with fanned napkins and gold rimmed service plates make this a romantic as well as a scenic place to dine.

The Mill Falls salad, topped with creamy Caesar-style dressing, is as fine a house salad as you'll find anywhere, but the French onion soup tastes as though it emerged from a package. I have no complaints about the moist, crumb-topped scrod but the calf's liver lyonnaise almost drowned in a pool of butter. The dinner menu features such Continental classics as prime rib, beef Wellington, and chateaubriand for two. Make sure you save room for dessert because the strawberry shortcake is made with good, old-fashioned biscuit.

Don't feel badly if inclement weather prevents you from dining on the sunny terrace. The dining room offers the elegance of mauve walls hung with silk hangings, Queen Anne chairs, and a changing exhibition of prints from the prestigious Pucker-Saffrai Gallery on Newbury Street. The service sets a standard for courtesy which snooty downtown waiters would do well to try to live up to.

PANACHE

Rating: ★★★★

Type of cuisine: contemporary/*nouvelle cuisine*

Price range: appetizers $3.25–5.95; entrees from $15.95–20.95

798 Main St., Cambridge

Telephone: 492–9500

Hours: open for lunch Thursday and Friday noon–2 p.m.; for dinner Tuesday–Saturday from 6–10 p.m.

Reservations recommended

Major credit cards accepted

Wine only

Wheelchair access good

Dress: jacket and tie

The concepts must have seemed revolutionary when the restaurant opened in 1978: the stark storefront dining room, the unusual flavor combinations such as duckling with sturgeon or tuna with sun-dried tomatoes, the measured, artful portions that left robust appetites wondering what was for dinner. Today, the restaurant Panache still delights and surprises because its talented, young chef, Bruce Frankel, has managed to stay one step ahead of Boston's culinary avant garde.

Frankel's secret lies in applying the tenets of French *nouvelle cuisine* (innovative recipes, starchless reduction sauces, painterly plate presentations) to an international array of ingredients. On one evening (the menu changes every three days), Maine lobster might be served with ginger and homemade pasta. On another, rack of lamb might be smoked on the premises to be accompanied by fresh herbs and zinfandel sauce. On special request, chef Frankel will prepare a *menu dégustation* ("tasting menu") enabling a couple to share small portions of 4 to 6 individual appetizers and entrees. Not to be missed is the Grand Dessert Panache, a medley of dessert specialties that includes a luscious chocolate *marquis* (mousse cake) with coffee sauce prepared by pastry chef Margaret Farl and served on a giant plate.

Located in a Central Square storefront, Panache attracts an almost cult-like following. The dining room, done in pinks and greys, boasts plush armchairs, lavish flower sprays, and an unusual pattern projector that casts seasonal images on the wall. Dinner with wine will run $40.00 per person but lunch at this chic Cambridge restaurant is surprisingly reasonable.

RITZ-CARLTON DINING ROOM

Rating: ★★★

Type of cuisine: Continental

Price range: appetizers $5.00–32.00 (average $8.00); entrees from $12.00–34.00

15 Arlington St., Boston

Telephone: 536–5700

Hours: open for lunch 7 days a week from noon–2:30 p.m.; for dinner Sunday–Thursday from 6–10:00 p.m., Friday and Saturday 6–11:00 p.m.

Reservations recommended

Major credit cards accepted

Full bar

Wheelchair access adequate

Entertainment: piano music evenings

Dress: jacket and tie

For 55 years, the Ritz-Carlton dining room has been *the* place to see and be seen by Boston's blue-blooded movers and shakers. But until quite recently, my praise was indeed begrudging of this admittedly elegant dining room with its staid Continental menu and insufferably snobbish staff. "Go to the Ritz for the scenery," I would say, "for the gold filigree ceilings, crystal chandeliers, potted palms, tinkling baby grand, and stunning view of the swan boats in the Boston Botanical Garden. You won't find me returning soon to a place where a waiter had the nerve to challenge my complaint that a mercilessly well-done lamb chop was improperly cooked!"

Return I did, however, and a recent lunch at the Ritz has forced me to reconsider both the classical Continental food and the black tie service. For who could contest a meal that included a velvet smooth vichyssoise (served in silver on ice), buttery, fresh soft-shelled crabs, and steak tartare prepared with artistry at the tableside. True, $10.50 seems steep for an avocado filled with crabmeat but the shellfish was as sweet as cream and topped with cognac mayonnaise. True the caviar costs $30, but how many restaurants serve authentic beluga on the back of an ice sturgeon with the classic garnish of hard-cooked egg, capers, onions, and neatly trimmed toast points? Other Ritz specialties include succulent duckling with cherries, cloudlike sweetbreads, and a pastry tray the mere sight of which is enough to make you salivate. Old wines are decanted in a machine that looks like a medieval torture device and coffee is poured from silver pots emblazoned with the double lion crest.

The formal dining room at the Ritz-Carlton is only part of the story because breakfast in the Ritz Café and drinks in the Ritz Bar are as legendary as the dining room. The former isn't much better than that at a good greasy spoon, it just tastes that way seasoned as it is by the sidewalk view of bustling Newbury St. The latter deserves mention for its lamp-lit marble tables and estimable, icy martinis. High tea is served daily in the upstairs lounge. Unique to the Ritz are the cobalt blue water glasses and flower-filled swan-shaped vases which grace the well-spaced tables.

SEASONS RESTAURANT

Rating: ★★★½

Type of cuisine: contemporary

Price range: appetizers $5.50–30.00; entrees $17.00–27.00

In the Bostonian Hotel, North & Blackstone Sts., Boston

Telephone: 523-3600

Hours: breakfast served daily from 7–10:30 a.m.; lunch from 11:30 a.m.–2:30 p.m.; for dinner Sunday–Thursday 6–10 p.m.; Friday and Saturday from 6–11 p.m.; and Saturday–Sunday brunch from 11:30 a.m.–3 p.m.

Reservations recommended

Major credit cards accepted

Full bar

Wheelchair access good

Dress: suit or jacket and tie

It used to be that hotel restaurants were shunned by all but the most unadventurous guests. Chefs Jasper White and Lydia Shire seem determined to prove, however, that fine hotel dining is alive and well at the Seasons Restaurant in the new Bostonian Hotel. Inspired by a grassroots movement sweeping the nation's top restaurants, the pair have applied the light-handed cooking techniques of French *nouvelle cuisine* and the Orient to the food specialties of their native New England. Their efforts have already fetched rave reviews, making the Seasons a popular restaurant not just with in-house guests but also the locals.

As the name of the restaurant and the changing charming watercolor on the menu suggest, the Season's bill of fare changes four times yearly. The chef's commitment to New England ingredients can be seen in such house specialties as Vermont smoked ham with pears poached in red wine, Cape Cod oysters broiled with herbs and spinach, *osetra* caviar (large-grained sturgeon eggs) served with Rhode Island johnnycakes, and the Bostonian seafood trilogy of broiled bay scallops, lobster-spinach roll and sesame seed-sprinkled bluefish.

This is not to say that the kitchen frowns on international cooking. The new *miso* (soybean paste) soup with salmon ravioli and the crisp duckling with scallion pancake (the duck breast is served rare, like steak) lend an Oriental flavor to the dinner selections. Desserts range from fancy French chocolate *charlotte* and *tonille aux peches* (hazelnut pastry with peaches) to a stunning sherbet sampler and traditional Key lime pie. The freshly ground coffee comes in a silver coffee pot and the decaffeinated coffee is made with real beans, not Sanka.

Located on the fourth floor of the Bostonian Hotel (you ascend in a glass elevator), the Season's dining room affords a spectacular view of the Faneuil Hall Marketplace and the business district through windowed walls and arched ceilings. (An ingenious electric curtain is used in daylight to shield diners from the incoming sun.) Built on graceful curves, the dining room bespeaks luxury, from the Louis XV-style chairs covered with marble-patterned fabric to the gleaming silver bell jars covering the entrees. The Seasons' wine list is devoted exclusively to American vintages, a Boston rarity. The service manages to be professional without being unfriendly or pompous (although some people have complained that it is slow).

The main drawback of the Seasons, indeed of most hotel restaurants, is its considerable expense. Lunch is marginally less expensive than dinner but I feel that dinner is the wiser investment. Perhaps the best compromise is to come for Sunday brunch which features the most unusual corned beef hash in town (the ingredients are cooked in colorful chunks, rather than ground to an unrecognizable pulp.)

UPSTAIRS AT THE PUDDING

Rating: ★★★½

Type of cuisine: Northern Italian

Price range: appetizers $4.50–6.00; entrees from $16.00–25.00

10 Holyoke St., Cambridge

Telephone: 864–1933

Hours: open for dinner Tuesday–Saturday from 6–10 p.m.

Reservations recommended

Major credit cards accepted

Full bar

Wheelchair access poor

Dress: suit or jacket and tie

This chic Italian restaurant opened with a bang—a reception for Ella Fitzgerald, who received the Hasty Pudding Woman of the Year award here in 1982. Its unique setting and unusual food are sure to keep the kudos and customers coming. Located on the top floor of the historic Hasty Pudding Club building off Harvard Square (gaze at the portraits of the five club members who became United States presidents as you mount the stairs), Upstairs at the Pudding offers the elegance of cantilevered ceiling timbers, forest green walls, and well-spaced tables set with pink cloths and gleaming brass service plates. The walls are decorated with playbills from the Hasty Pudding theatricals and on performance evenings you can hear the clarion calls of trumpets from the stage downstairs. The theatrics aren't limited to the setting, however, and the "Pudding" vies with Allegro (see p. 3) in Waltham as the top Italian restaurant in town.

Pudding chef Michael Silver, formerly of the Peasant Stock, as is his partner, Mary Catherine Deibel, applies the cooking techniques of Northern Italy and the studied plate presentations of French nouvelle cuisine to an international array of ingredients. You could start your dinner with homemade *tagliatelli* (ribbon-like egg noodles) garnished with frogs' legs or, perhaps, hand-rolled *tortellini* (pasta dumplings) filled with escargots and ricotta. The Pudding is one of the only restaurants in town that serves *abbacchio* (milk-fed "hothouse" lamb). Other entrees from the daily-changing menu include imported French turbot with almond and sherry sauce and beef tenderloin topped with goose liver and fresh black truffles. Accompanying each entree is a stunning array of as many as six different vegetables, ranging from fried sage leaves to cardoon (a thistle-like plant in the artichoke family) to salsify (a white root whose moist consistency has earned it the nickname "oyster plant"). Desserts are equally exotic, running from passion fruit *granita* (an icy sherbet) to an un-Italian chocolate-macadamia nut tart.

The Pudding wine list harbors such choice Italian reds as Monsecco (from the Gatinara district), Taurasi (from Campania in Central Italy), and Amaroni (a powerful wine made from partially dried grapes). The cheese tray, garlanded with fresh flowers, does justice to the lesser known but excellent goat and triple cream cheeses of the Italian peninsula. The meal begins with complimentary olives and roasted peppers and ends with amarone cookies which accompany the check. After dinner you can take the evening air watching the street performers in Harvard Square.

VOYAGERS

Rating: ★★★

Type of cuisine: French/contemporary

Price range: appetizers \$4.50–6.50; entrees \$16.00–20.00

45 Mount Auburn St., Cambridge

Telephone: 354–1718

Hours: open for dinner Tuesday–Saturday from 6–9:30 p.m.

Reservations mandatory

Major credit cards accepted

Full bar

Wheelchair access fair

Entertainment: live harp music nightly

Dress: suit or jacket and tie

One could say that the Voyagers Restaurant exists for the sake of its wine cellar. The wine list boasts 400 different vintages, ranging from a priceless 1874 Chateaux Lafite to an excellent selection of California boutique wines. Most red wines are served in crystal decanters and all are drunk from gorgeous hand-blown goblets. The Voyagers sells homemade wine vinegar and T-shirts emblazoned with emblems of vineyards. Even the restroom walls are plastered with vintage wine labels.

To visit the Voyagers for the wine alone, however, would be to overlook one of the most spectacular restaurant settings and estimable cuisines in Cambridge. Where else can guests dine beneath the stars in a rooftop greenhouse complete with bonsai garden and murmuring fountain? How many other restaurants pamper their guests with individually calligraphed place settings? Non-smokers have their own dining room; and all dining areas are graced with gallery-quality Oriental and contemporary art.

A kindred meticulousness characterizes the kitchen where art gallery owner-turned-chef Dorothy Koval smokes her own game birds, cultivates fresh herbs and even candies her own rose petals for garnishing desserts. Koval's sense of humor appears in such fanciful creations as scallops *en voyage* (in a pastry boat festooned with a parchment sail) and fettuccini Moors and Christians (garnished with black olives and white truffles).

The bill of fare changes daily; a recent Valentine's Day menu included artichokes Voyagers (stuffed with mushroom *duxelles* and topped with hollandaise sauce), beef tournedos Saint Amant (served with apples, liver pâté and port sauce in puff pastry), and gâteau marjolaine (a dizzyingly rich confection of nut meringue with chocolate, vanilla, and hazelnut buttercream). The homemade bread is as buttery as can be.

The live harp and harpsichord music makes the Voyagers one of Boston's most romantic restaurants. My only complaint is the restaurant's lack of consistency: when the food is good, it is very, very good; when it is not, it is commonplace.

A SQUARE MEAL FOR A FAIR DEAL

Boston's Best Mid-Priced Restaurants

ANTHONY'S PIER 4

Rating: ★★

Type of cuisine: seafood

Price range: appetizers $2.50–5.00; entrees $6.00–25.00

140 Northern Avenue, Boston

Telephone: 482–6262

Hours: Monday–Friday from 11:30 a.m.–11 p.m.; Saturday noon–11 p.m.; Sunday from 12:30 p.m.–10 p.m.

No reservations

Major credit cards accepted

Full bar

Wheelchair access adequate

Dress: jacket and tie

Anthony's Pier 4 is the seafood restaurant Bostonians love to hate. They hate it because it is a food factory, processing as many as 1,600 dinners an evening. They hate it because you can't make reservations and a Saturday night dinner necessitates a 40- to 60-minute wait. They hate it because the seafood is not always as fresh as it should be at a restaurant built on a pier in Boston Harbor. Yet for all these shortcomings, they flock here in droves, making Anthony's Pier 4 the highest grossing, privately owned restaurant in the country.

    The Pier 4 stands as a tribute to one Anthony Athanas, an Albanian immigrant who started as a shoeshine boy, built a restaurant and then a seafood empire—there are four Anthony restaurants in greater Boston.

The sheer dimensions of Pier 4 boggle the mind; the parking lot is the size of several football fields and each of the two dining rooms seats 600. In the old days, no politician or movie star would come to Boston without visiting Anthony's—their photos plaster the entryway and lounge. Today, the waiters wear cutesy colonial buckskins and knee breeches to remind us of Boston's history.

Anthony's starts out strong with complimentary hors d'oeuvres, well-garnished halfshell items, freshly baked popovers and a delicious Caesar-style house salad. Entrees can be problematic, however, ranging from dry broiled fish to rubbery seafood casseroles, but you can't go wrong with the Boston scrod, a small fish in the cod family, broiled with a buttery topping of breadcrumbs. Desserts include a superior Indian pudding and ice cream pie with hot lemon sauce.

Anthony's Pier 4 has what is probably the best wine list in Boston, boasting an unsurpassed selection of California vintages and honeyed dessert wines sold by the half bottle. Don't forget to wear jackets and neckties, gentlemen, or you will not be admitted.

Like Locke-Ober's and Durgin-Park, Anthony's is a Boston institution. There is better seafood elsewhere but this landmark deserves at least one visit.

BANGKOK CUISINE

Rating: ★★½

Type of cuisine: Thai

Price range: appetizers $2.00–4.00; entrees from $5.00–9.00

177A Massachusetts Ave., Boston

Telephone: 262–5377

Hours: open for lunch Monday–Friday from 11:30 a.m.–3 p.m., for dinner from 5–10:30 p.m., for dinner Saturday–Sunday from 5–10 p.m.

No reservations

Major credit cards accepted

Beer and wine

Wheelchair access good

Dress: casual

A meal at Bangkok Cuisine is felt as much as it is tasted. It begins as a burning sensation that sears your tongue and blasts your throat and sinuses. Your brow pearls with sweat and if you order a particularly spicy dish, it even makes you perspire under your eyelids! Water will not quench it although beer, preferably hopsy Singha beer from Thailand, does provide temporary relief. It is called "chili hellfire" and, paradoxically, the best way to soothe it is to take another mouthful!

Using the fiery seasonings of India, the stir-fry cooking of China, and a host of exotic ingredients such as salty fish sauce, fragrant lemon grass, and creamy coconut pulp, the Thais have evolved one of the world's great cuisines, a cuisine I would rank with French, Japanese, and Italian for its sensory adventure. It comes as no surprise, then, that one of my all-time favorite Boston restaurants is Bangkok Cuisine, located on Mass. Ave. near Symphony Hall, the Berklee Performance Center, and the Christian Science Mother Church.

Classic Thai appetizers include *sate* (char-broiled beef kebabs) and *tod mun pla* (deep-fried bluefish patties), the latter served with a chili-laced vinegar-cucumber saucer for dipping. Thai soups range from alluring *tom yum nur* (beef soup flavored with tart lime juice, pungent coriander leaf, and perfumy galengale—a root related to ginger) to a chicken coconut soup that is so sweet and creamy it could almost double as a dessert.

Gluttons for punishment will like the red shrimp curry (shellfish, green beans, and peppers in a creamy, hot coconut sauce), "duck 'n chili" (when they say "hot," they mean it!), and *pla rad prik* (a spectacular whole fried bass topped with chili sauce and mushrooms). Among the less spicy dishes are Thai fried rice and *pad thai*, the national dish of Thailand made with fried noodles and loaded with peanuts, shrimp, and vegetables. When ordering the latter, be sure to ask for the condiment tray so as to whet your tongue on the pickled chilis.

Bangkok Cuisine is a pretty restaurant, its narrow dining room graced with a stained glass skylight and sparkling chandelier. Folk paintings of Thailand adorn the walls and table tops are embellished with shadow puppets sandwiched between red cloths and glass tops. The waiters used to be more gracious when the restaurant first opened but they are still more friendly than those in most restaurants in Chinatown. Expect a wait if you dine at Bangkok Cuisine during peak hours, as the 50-seat dining room is far too small to accommodate the restaurant's loyal following.

BRANDY PETE'S

Rating: ★★

Type of cuisine: homestyle (American/Italian/Continental)

Price range: entrees from $4.25–11.00

82 Broad St., Boston

Telephone: 482–4165

Hours: open Monday–Friday from 11:30 a.m.–9 p.m.

No reservations

No credit cards

Full bar

Wheelchair access good

Dress: casual to jacket and tie

The original Brandy Pete was a cantankerous old coot who bought himself a brandy at the customer's expense whenever the latter complained, stayed away from the restaurant too long, or even brought in new clients. ("More damn work," Pete would mutter.) The customers loved it then, they love it now, and although the original Pete is long gone, this boisterous bar and restaurant still draws lunchtime crowds of as many as 300. Some of the waitresses (more demure than those at Durgin-Park) have been here for 25 years; so have some of the customers; and should an old timer fail to show up at his appointed hour, you can be certain that someone from the restaurant will call to make sure that he is OK. As for Brandy Pete, "He was the only person I ever knew who was a legend," says one customer. "Why I must have bought him 500 brandies," laughs another.

That is not to say that this home-style restaurant in the heart of the financial district has not kept pace with the present. Lunchtime draws an older business crowd, but at dinner Brandy Pete's fills with a youngish crowd from the Waterfront. Now, as in the old days, the crudely typed menu lists more than 60 items, ranging from homemade chicken pot pie and "Atlantic Ave. fish stew" to such dishes as chicken *cacciatore* and spaghetti and meatballs which reflect the Italian heritage of the Sabia family. Much of the bill of fare changes daily but the braised lamb shanks, broiled bluefish, and grapenut pudding remain perennial favorites. The food at Brandy Pete's makes up for its lack of finesse by the generosity of its portions. The two-fisted drinks, among them bone-dry martinis, are legendary.

The cavernous, cream-colored dining room, with its wooden booths and tables decked with checkered tablecloths, has changed very little since Pius "Pete" Sabia opened the restaurant in 1943. Although Pete passed away over ten years ago, there are reminders of him everywhere, from a cigar-toting portrait that includes his favorite motto ("The customer is always wrong!") to menus inscribed with such Brandy Pete aphorisms as, "A bird in the hand should be house-broken," and "He always omits the 'r' when he spells burocrat."

CAFE CALYPSO

Rating: ★★½

Type of cuisine: contemporary

Price range: appetizers $3.00–5.00; entrees $8.00–10.00

578 Tremont St., Boston

Telephone: 267–7228

Hours: open Tuesday–Saturday 8 a.m.–11 p.m.; Sunday brunch 11 a.m.–3 p.m.

No reservations

Major credit cards accepted

Beer and wine

Wheelchair access fair

Dress: casual

The Calypso of Greek mythology was an enchantress who kept Odysseus captive for seven years on her island. Boston's Café Calypso is an enchantress of a different sort; a chic South End café/restaurant that has captured a loyal local following with its robust soups, refined pastries, and surprisingly reasonable prices.

Opened by former C'est Si Bon baker Franco Campanello, the Café Calypso specializes in all manner of breads, pies, tortes, and mouth-watering pastries. No North End pizzeria could match Franco's *calzone* (cheese and sausage-filled turnovers) and I doubt that there is a better quiche anywhere this side of Lorraine. Calypso's salads are copious and imaginative and the cheese trays, prettily festooned with a bird cut from an apple, always include a *chèvre* (French goat cheese). Hot entrees range from stuffed Cornish game hen to wonderfully garlicky scampi. But whatever you order here, save room for the magnificent desserts such as mincemeat pie that will set you longing for Thanksgiving, and Linzertorte, filled with black currants and crème de cassis, that will bring a smile to the lips of anyone who samples it.

In order to accommodate an ever-growing clientele, Calypso owner Campanello has added a second dining room. The decor remains eclectic, ranging from purple tabletops and white art deco lamps to paneled walls and lavender ceilings. A small wine list boasts reasonably priced vintages. A waist-high showcase separates the dining area from the kitchen so you can savor the sights and smells of your food as it is being prepared.

CALLAHAN'S

Rating: ★★½

Type of cuisine: meat and potatoes

Price range: appetizers from $2.75; entrees $4.50–11.00

100 Needham St., Newton

Telephone: 527–0330

131 Boston Post Rd., Wayland

Telephone: 358–7741

Hours: open seven days a week from 11 a.m.–11 p.m.

No reservations

No credit cards

Full bar

Wheelchair access adequate

Dress: casual

"I don't believe you should chisel the customer," says Bill Farral, general manager of Callahan's. Founded by one John Callahan, this west suburb steak house chain has been drawing capacity crowds with its low prices and huge portions since the Newton branch opened in 1950. The bargains begin in the bar where the drinks come in tumblers so large you almost need both hands to raise them to your lips. (The markup on wine here is 30%—around $2 per bottle—as opposed to the 200% charged by most restaurants.) Undoubtedly you can find a more tender steak elsewhere but few restaurants give you more meal for the money.

Unlike most steak houses, Callahan's serves excellent appetizers, ranging from fried mozzarella sticks that form long strings of cheese as you lift them from the mustard dipping sauce to deep-fried potato skins served with spicy cheddar cheese dip that were voted the best fried spud skins in Greater Boston in a recent *Globe Calendar Magazine*. A creamy vinaigrette dressing accompanies the house salad (sold à la carte as are all the vegetables), while "Callahan's potatoes," consisting of potato eighths cooked crisp and brown in the fryer, are simply the best steak fries I have had anywhere. But the star attraction here is the beef—top choice with a "Y4" fat quotient (meat is graded Y1 through 6 according to its fat content, Y6 being the most marbled and tender). Steaks are aged for five days before being cooked under a special infrared broiler that sears in the juices. Meat cuts include filet mignon (the most tender), Delmonico steaks (from the rib eye), sirloin (from the strip), and "New York sirloin" (the toughest—from the rump). Burgers, served on onion kaiser rolls, are equally well-charred and juicy.

To judge from the crowds that nightly queue up for a table (no reservations), Callahan's needs no formal introduction. The bar at the Newton Callahan's has a lively social scene and the seven-year-old Wayland branch seats 230 customers at formica tables beneath whirling paddle fans. The cheesecake is a little lackluster but the ice cream sundaes never fail to please.

CARL'S PAGODA

Rating: ★★½

Type of cuisine: Chinese (Cantonese)

Price range: appetizers $3.25–6.50; entrees $5.00–14.00

23 Tyler St., Boston

Telephone: 357–9837

Hours: open for dinner seven days a week from 5–12 p.m.

Reservations accepted on weekdays

No credit cards

BYOB

Wheelchair access poor

Dress: casual

This Cantonese restaurant has a clientele inversely proportional to the dimensions of its tiny dining room. The faithful maintain that you should never look at the menu but rather base your dinner on whatever Carl recommends that particular evening. Carl is the middle-aged, bespectacled man sitting at the rear table wearing a neck tie, smoking cigarettes and staring into space (or over his dominion). Whenever I have dined at the Pagoda, it's not Carl but his septuagenarian uncle who takes the orders and does the serving. The latter, whom customers affectionately call "grandpa," speaks with a heavy accent so finding out just what Carl recommends can be kind of tricky. Do persist, however, because the kitchen serves some of the lightest, freshest, tastiest fare in Chinatown.

If you ask Carl, or grandpa, what he recommends, chances are he will name Carl's soup, Carl's clams, or shrimp or lobster with scallions and ginger. The first is a tomato-based version of egg drop soup, the second consists of a dozen and a half clams steamed with spicy black bean sauce, and the third combines the striking flavors of garlic and ginger with the pearly delicacy of shellfish. (You don't really have to ask Carl, anyway, as all three items are on the menu!) To one of the above add an order of the audibly crisp fried wontons, served with homemade mustard and duck sauce, and a noodle dish, or perhaps beef with black beans (the meat can be tough, however), and you've got yourself a first rate Cantonese dinner. Hot tea and water come without asking but beer and wine must be brought in the proverbial brown bag.

Located on the second floor of an apartment building on a side street in Chinatown, Carl's Pagoda is easy to miss unless you know exactly where you are going. Look for a red facade and steep steps. The no-frills dining room holds 11 red formica tables which—a nice touch—are set with linen napkins. The decor is limited to prints and a few Chinese lanterns. It takes a while to warm up to the staff, then again, that's pretty much the rule for Chinatown.

CHEF CHANG'S HOUSE

Rating: ★★

Type of cuisine: Chinese (Mandarin-Szechuan)

Price range: appetizers $2.00–4.50; entrees $5.00–18.00 (average $5.00–7.00)

1004–1006 Beacon St., Brookline

Telephone: 277–4226

Hours: open seven days a week, noon to 9:30 p.m.

Reservations for parties of 8 or more

Major credit cards accepted

Full bar

Wheelchair access good

Dress: nice casual

A wizened, smiling Chinese chef in a white jacket wheels a steaming serving cart to your table. On it is one of the glories of Chinese gastronomy: a glistening, whole Peking duck. The day before, the skin was painstakingly loosened from the bird and dried to make it crisp and fatless. The head and feet have been left on as visible proof that the fowl was poultry farm fresh.

Wielding a razor-sharp cleaver, the chef carves the bird into a neat pile of crisp skin and anise-spiced duck meat. Meanwhile, the waiter serves platters of crepe-like pancakes, tangy hoisin sauce, and scallion brushes: the name of the game is to make a Peking duck "sandwich" with the skin, duck, and crepes, painting the pancake with sauce, and gobbling the scallion "paintbrush" with it. Welcome to Chef Chang's

House, where Peking duck is the house specialty, and where, unlike at most Chinese restaurants, this extravagant dish is served seven nights a week without the inconvenience of advance ordering.

Chef Chang's House opened in 1981 at a storefront in what is rapidly becoming Brookline's "restaurant row" (Brown's Steak House and the Sol Azteca are its immediate neighbors). Everything about this restaurant sets it apart from its Chinatown counterparts. No lurid formica here, but two spacious dining areas (non-smokers will appreciate having their own room) decorated with festive lanterns, textured wall paper, and graceful brush paintings. Guests take their seats on bentwood chairs at tables graced with cloths and linen napkins. Even the service is uncommonly civil!

Chef Chang specializes in the cooking of Northern and Eastern China, proposing such delicacies as Hunan pork with spicy black bean sauce and gingery General Gau's chicken. The chef's flair for theatrics is apparent in the serving of the sizzling rice soup (it roars like a volcano) and the spicy, crispy cod, a whole fried fish topped with pork sauce (the eyes have been masked with maraschino cherries to spare the squeamish). Equally impressive are the eight-course Chinese banquets (available to groups of eight or more), which are served in a private dining area.

These attractions have made Chef Chang's one of the area's most popular Chinese restaurants, so expect a wait on a Friday or Saturday evening. The bar serves Polynesian-style cocktails as well as Western vintages.

CHEZ NOUS

Rating: ★★★

Type of cuisine: nouvelle cuisine

Price range: appetizers $3.00–5.00; entrees $15.00–20.00

147 Huron Ave., Cambridge

Telephone: 864–6670

Hours: open for dinner Tuesday–Saturday from 6–9:30 p.m.

Reservations recommended for the dining room; seats on the terrace available on a first come, first served basis

Major credit cards accepted

BYOB

Wheelchair access good

Dress: jacket and tie or turtleneck

Some people are drawn here by the outdoor terrace, a charming space faced with barnboard and slate paving stones and shaded by a canopy of twice-blooming wisteria. Others favor the dining room, with its trellised ceiling, clean white walls, shuttered windows, and intimate seating for thirty. A third group likes this charming restaurant for the one thing it lacks—a wine license. (There are all too few fine restaurants where a wine buff can bring his own prized vintages.)

All of these virtues would be for naught, however, without the estimable cooking of owner-chef Elizabeth Fischer, who applies the common sense of American health food cookery to the starchless reduction sauces and unusual flavor combinations of French nouvelle cuisine.

The menu changes weekly, boasting innovations such as red pepper bisque alongside Mediterranean classics such as *filetto carpaccio* (sliced, uncooked beef tenderloin served with tangy caper-herb sauce). Main courses are an exercise in counterpoint: the sweetness of figs balanced by the saltiness of Roquefort cheese in a stuffed chicken breast, or lamb served with a sauce made from fruity *balsamic* vinegar and piquant Pommery mustard. Vegetables are cooked briefly enough to preserve their bright colors without being so *al dente* that you need both hands to cut them. As for dessert, although chef Fischer hails from Munich, her walnut spice torte and ethereal almond cake with raspberry sauce display true Viennese finesse.

This cozy, North Cambridge storefront has sheltered a number of precocious restaurants including Le Bocage and Le Beau Geste, where Fischer served as chef. Its atmosphere combines the casual comfort of a neighborhood eatery with the elegance of a chic boutique restaurant. The one problem—as is the case with most storefront restaurants—is that there is no place to wait if your table is not ready, which makes seated guests feel rushed and standing guests feel impatient. The answer lies in both the management and the customers heeding the precise times of their reservations.

CYBELE ON THE WATERFRONT

Rating: ★★★

Type of cuisine: contemporary/Continental

Price range: appetizers $2.50–6.00; entrees $13.00–19.00

240 Commercial St., Boston

Telephone: 523–1126

Hours: open for dinner Tuesday–Saturday from 5:30–11 p.m.; Sunday till 10 p.m.; Sunday brunch from 11 a.m.–3 p.m.

Reservations recommended

Major credit cards accepted

Full bar

Wheelchair access adequate

Dress: jacket and tie or turtleneck

The mercurial Rebecca Caras has certainly had her ups and downs in the restaurant business. At one point her empire included a catering service, gourmet carry-out shops in Cambridge and Faneuil Hall, and a pair of much-touted restaurants. At this writing, Caras is concentrating her efforts on her Charles St. café and fancy downtown restaurant and no survey of the Boston food scene would be complete without a visit to Cybele on the Waterfront.

Caras describes the food at Cybele as "eclectic seasonal," uniting classic French cooking techniques with the bold flavors of the Mediterranean and the health consciousness of the 80's. The appetizers belie Caras' Greek heritage, running from spinach turnovers (wrapped in filo dough) and homemade lamb sausage to uncommonly flavorful pâté. Typical Cybele entrees include fish-stew like *cioppino*, tournedos Hemingway (with oysters), and venison medallions with pomegranate-port sauce.

For me, however, the restaurant's star attraction is the Sunday brunch. In a town where bland chafing-dish fare is the norm, Cybele's buffet retains the pristine freshness of a homemade breakfast. The chicken and almond salad is good, the fresh, meticulously peeled asparagus with tarragon sauce is better, and the chicken livers with apples and all-you-can-eat smoked salmon will send you back to the buffet line for seconds. Even the carrot cake has a finesse seldom found elsewhere.

Cybele on the Waterfront is a gorgeous restaurant done in cool shades of grey, pink, and turquoise that are remarkable in their relaxing, sedative effect on the customers. The main dining room boasts tiers, brick walls, and exposed ceiling beams while a second room, with its mirrored walls and swag curtains affords a distant view of the harbor. (This room is often reserved for private parties.) The art is original, ranging from contemporary canvases to arty black and white photographs. The serving staff, dressed in their starched white tuxedo shirts, gives no cause for complaint. Another plus is that Cybele on the Waterfront serves a supper menu of sandwiches, pasta, and other light fare.

O FADO

Rating: ★★½

Type of cuisine: Portuguese

Price range: appetizers $2.00–4.50; entrees $7.00–10.00

72 Walnut St., Peabody

Telephone: 531–9687

Hours: open seven days a week from 11 a.m.–11 p.m.

Reservations accepted

No credit cards

Full bar

Wheelchair access good

Entertainment: Portuguese music and dancing every Friday and Saturday

Dress: casual

The town of Peabody is not what you would call a gastronomic capital but this one-time textile center, home to a sizable Portuguese community descended from leather workers, boasts an outstanding Portuguese restaurant called O Fado. To find it, you drive past a long, bleak stretch of warehouses and turn in at the sign of the banjo-playing maiden. O Fado is a friendly, working class bar and restaurant; the sort of place where regulars will lean over to tell newcomers what to order. Red cloths drape the tables and the barnboard walls are decorated with lobster claw gnomes and giant photographs of Portuguese bullfights. The object of a Portuguese bullfight, by the way, is not for the matador to kill the bull but simply to pull its tail!

Flanked by the Atlantic, Portugal has long been a seafaring nation and the popularity of seafood here is matched only by that of spices from the distant strands conquered by the early Portuguese explorers. Seafood figures prominently on O Fado's bilingual menu, ranging from *ameijoa a bolhao* (littlenecks cooked with parsley and olive oil) to *camarao com molho de alho* (pan-fried shrimp laced with tabasco sauce and garlic). Shellfish fans should order the *mariscada com mohlo verde* (shrimp, clams, scallops, and a whole lobster served directly in the pot in which they were simmered). But seafood is only half the story because the *linguica* (spicy sausage) comes flamed with brandy and the *codorniz* (marinated, grilled quail) are as tender and tasty as can be. Other Portuguese specialties here include *carne de porco a alentejana* (pork stewed with clams) and a sweet, eggy *flan* (caramel custard) for dessert.

The country that invented port wine obviously takes its drinking seriously and at O Fado you will find not only refreshing Portuguese wines (try the sparkling white Aveleda) but also *Aniz*, a licoricy after-dinner drink, and *Maracuja*, a potent passion-fruit liqueur. A *fado* is a Portuguese folk song, by the way, and on the weekends the restaurant features live music and dancing.

GENJI

Rating: ★★★

Type of cuisine: Japanese

Price range: appetizers $2.00–6.00; entrees $8.00–15.00

327 Newbury St., Boston

Telephone: 267–5656

Hours: Monday–Thursday 11:30–2:30 p.m. and 5:30–10:30 p.m.; Friday 11:30–2:30 and 5:30–11:00 p.m.; Saturday 12:00–3:00 and 5:30–11:00 p.m.; Sunday 4:30–10:00 p.m.

Reservations recommended

Major credit cards accepted

Full bar

Wheelchair access good

Dress: jacket and tie to casual

Upstairs, a swashbuckling chef sautées shrimp and steak on a *teppan* (specially heated) table. Downstairs, another chef slices razor-thin ribbons of tuna, salmon, and pickled mackerel to make jewel-like vinegared rice cakes called *sushi.* Welcome to Genji, one of Boston's oldest and best Japanese restaurants where age-old Oriental delicacies are served with contemporary Newbury Street savvy.

Named for a royal family of 12th century Kyoto, Genji offers three traditional Japanese dining experiences. The ground floor harbors several *teppan* rooms, where bandannaed chefs perform a floor show as they sauté *sukiyaki* directly on your table. (The tables seat eight so it's best to bring a large group lest you wind up dining with strangers.) Downstairs, there is a sushi bar (reservations recommended), where you can watch the preparation of *sashimi* (uncooked fish platter) and *sushi,* garnished with such briny delicacies as *hamachi* (yellow-tail), *tako* (octopus), and *tekka* (tuna rolled with rice and crinkly seaweed). To eat *sashimi* and *sushi,* pour a little soy sauce into the saucer provided and season it with *wasabi,* spicy Japanese horseradish, which looks like a dab of green toothpaste. Use chopsticks for *sashimi,* your fingers for *sushi,* dipping the seafood into the soy sauce before eating. By the way, the mound of tan-colored ribbon on your plate is pickled ginger.

Genji also has regular tables at booths that are tastefully decorated with block prints and handsome *misu* screens. Other house specialties include *tempura* (batter-fried vegetables), and *nabe* (pot-cooked dinners) which are simmered to taste on hotplates installed on your table. Skip the Polynesian-style cocktails and order *sake,* hot rice wine served in thimble-sized cups. For dessert the ginger ice cream is a must.

GRILL 23

Rating: ★★★

Type of cuisine: meat and potatoes

Price range: appetizers $4.50–7.00; entrees $12.00–19.50

161 Berkeley St., Boston

Telephone: 542–2255

Hours: lunch Monday–Friday from 11:30 a.m.–2:30 p.m.; dinner seven days a week from 6–10 p.m. (late night supper from 10:30–midnight); Sunday brunch from 11 a.m.–3 p.m.

Reservations recommended

Major credit cards accepted

Full bar

Wheelchair access fair

Dress: jacket and tie

To judge from the overnight success of the Grill 23, a New York-style steak house was just what Boston needed. At this writing the Grill 23 has barely been open a week and already it is serving 80 people at midday and 200 people for dinner. Like any new restaurant, the Grill will experience growing pains (slow service and an occasional cold steak) but I predict that this stylish chop house will quickly become a Boston institution.

Like so many new restaurants, the Grill 23 has hopped on the back-to-New-England-cooking bandwagon. The grilled duckling is native; so are the scallops, scrod (grilled here, not baked with bread crumbs), and superior Indian pudding. The beef (available in every conceivable size and cut) acquires a superb flavor, aged as it is for three weeks and expertly charred over one of the restaurant's three grills. The sirloin is sliced like roast beef. Onions, mushrooms, and eggplant are available grilled, as are fresh pineapple slices served with ice cream (a combination that is truly delicious). The oysters Rockefeller are above average, the Caesar salad is excellent, and the Grill 23's cottage fries are cooked to order, not frozen, as is sadly the case at most Boston steak houses. One complaint: the calf's liver looked as though it had been sliced with a chain saw.

Located in the historic Salada Tea building in what used to be the city passport office, the Grill 23 offers the 1920's elegance of sculpted ceilings, burnished lamplights, and six massive polished marble pillars. The split level dining room has seating for 150 at tables set with snowy cloths, heavy silver, and marble salt and pepper shakers. I like the clubby mood created by the brass and mahogany that line the dining room and lounge area. A piece of carpet would help control the noise which is considerable.

HARVARD BOOKSTORE CAFE

Rating: ★★

Type of cuisine: contemporary/Continental/fingerfood

Price range: appetizers from $3.25–5.25; entrees $4.95–12.95

190 Newbury Street, Boston

Telephone: 536–0095

Hours: open for breakfast Monday–Saturday from 8–11 a.m.; for lunch Monday–Saturday from 11:30 a.m.–4:30 p.m.; for dinner Monday–Saturday from 5:30–10:30 p.m.

No reservations

Major credit cards accepted

Wine and beer

Wheelchair access adequate

Dress: casual

As a writer and also a cook, I have often dreamed of running a combination bookstore-restaurant. Frank Kramer, president of Harvard Bookstore, had exactly the same idea, so in May of 1980, he opened the Harvard Bookstore Café. Located on fashionable Newbury St., the Café serves a contemporary menu from early morning to late at night.

Breakfast features frothy cappuccino, warm muffins, and fresh croissants (the latter originally created by Viennese bakers to celebrate the defeat of the Turks—their emblem a crescent—in 1683). Lunch might include a generous *salade niçoise* (tuna, anchovies, string beans, and potatoes) or pasta *du jour*—made with imported Menucci noodles topped with cream and vegetables or, perhaps, with prosciutto and peas. Dinner entrees change daily and range from steak and kidney pie to scrod with lemon-caper butter. Fish is a particular point of pride for the Café with such under-utilized sea creatures as bluefish, tile fish, and monkfish featured frequently on the menu. The best news, however, is the pastry selection garnered from four separate sources, including Brookline's master *chocolatière* Carol Pollack. But as to which is superior, the "chocolate velvet" (spongecake filled with chocolate mousse, topped with dark chocolate glaze) or the Toulouse-Lautrec cake (a single layer of dense, thick, bittersweet chocolate cake served with a ruff of Grand Marnier-flavored whipped cream), I leave to you to decide.

Tucked behind book displays, the Café dining rooms boast a contemporary decor of butcher block tables, high-tech lights, and smartly framed lithographs. (If possible, sit in the front room as the split-level dining area in the back can make one feel a little claustrophobic.) Weather permitting, the prime seats in the house are those on the sidewalk terrace. The service may be a trifle leisurely but is certainly well-intentioned.

JONAH'S ON THE TERRACE AT THE HYATT REGENCY

Rating: ★★½

Type of cuisine: Sunday brunch/Continental

Price range: $15.50 for all you can eat ($10.50 for children under 10)

575 Memorial Drive, Cambridge

Telephone: 492–1234

Hours: open daily from 7 a.m.–10:30 p.m., Friday–Saturday till 11:30 p.m.; only brunch served on Sundays from 10 a.m.–3 p.m.

Reservations accepted for parties of 8 or more

Major credit cards accepted

Full bar

Wheelchair access adequate

Entertainment: nightly (live piano) in the adjacent Pallysadoe Lounge

Dress: jacket and tie or turtleneck

"Oh my, I've died and gone to heaven!" is a thought that springs to mind at the Sunday brunch at Jonah's on the Terrace at the Hyatt Regency in Cambridge. This all-you-can-eat buffet might well seem like earthly paradise with its glistening ice sculptures, sunny view of the boat-studded Charles River, and jazz combo playing discreetly on the balcony. Only Parker's at the Parker House and the Café Fleuri at the Hotel Meridien have brunch spreads that can rival the Hyatt's and, although Parker's dining room may be more imposing and the Meridien's cooking more pretentious, when it comes to the actual taste of the food, you will find me in line at the Hyatt.

And in line I will be, because from the moment Jonah's opens, crowds of brunch-goers make waiting for a table mandatory. Spend the time admiring the Hyatt's multi-story, glass enclosed atrium with its transparent elevators, murmuring fountains, and million-dollar collection of contemporary art and wall hangings. Once seated, you will be served freshly squeezed orange juice and coffee and invited to visit the lavish buffet as often as you like.

When making your way around the eight-sided buffet table, bear in mind that the best of the more than three dozen items are waiting for you at the end. Cast an eye (and surely a fork) at the attractive cold cut platters and chafing dishes loaded with scrambled eggs and blintzes, quiches, crepes, and breakfast meats. But be sure to save plenty of room for the Edenesque fruit display, freshly carved steamship round (served with tiny poppy seed rolls), and a smoked fish spread that includes all the hand-sliced smoked salmon you can eat. As at most hotels, the cakes and pastries look better than they actually taste but do load up on the fresh strawberries served with equally fresh whipped cream.

On Wednesday evenings, Jonah's brunch spread gives way to an all-you-can-eat seafood buffet. In addition to Jonah's, the Hyatt has two other restaurants, the Empress Room and the Spinnaker Lounge, both located on the top floor of the hotel. The former is a fancy Chinese restaurant whose astronomical prices are partially offset by the stunning view of downtown Boston from its tiered, glass-walled dining room. House specialties include lobster spring rolls, won ton consommé, Peking duck, and filet mignon with oysters and Chinese mushrooms. The same stunning view can be had for considerably less money at the revolving Spinnaker Lounge which serves lunch and a light evening menu daily.

LEGAL SEA FOODS

Rating: ★★★

Type of cuisine: seafood

Price range: appetizers $1.50–7.00; entrees $7.00–13.00 (higher for caviar and lobster)

5 Cambridge Center, Kendall Square, Cambridge

Telephone: 864–3400

Rte. 9, Chestnut Hill

Telephone: 277–7300

Boston Park Plaza Hotel, 35 Columbus Avenue, Boston

Telephone: 426–4444

Hours: open Monday–Saturday from 11 a.m.–10 p.m., Sunday noon–10 p.m.

No reservations

Major credit cards accepted

Full bar

Wheelchair access good

Dress: casual

"I got scrod last night for dinner," is a sentiment felt all too often by patrons of Boston fish houses. But seldom when they dine at Legal Sea Foods. For whether they ordered the moist fried clams, meaty broiled bluefish, Oriental sashimi, or traditional New England scrod, you can be sure they received the freshest fish in the city.

As befits a good seafood restaurant, Legal began as a fish market opened by George Berkowitz in Inman Square in Cambridge. By 1968, George was serving his rib-sticking chowder and crisp-fried haddock to crowds of Cambridge fish lovers who seemed oblivious to the long waiting lines and boisterous dinner guests jammed at communal tables. The success of the first Legal prompted the opening of a second restaurant at the Chestnut Hill Mall, this one graced with hanging plants and well-spaced tables. The third Legal, located in the Boston Park Plaza Hotel, achieved the elegance of a downtown dining establishment with its South Seas atmosphere complete with wicker chairs and brass railings. A Kendall Square Legal, opened to replace the Inman Square branch which burned down, has become the newest outpost of the Berkowitz empire and here, too, the family motto, "If it isn't fresh, it isn't legal," aptly characterizes the food.

Legal specialties include home-smoked bluefish pâté, stuffed mussels, and Alaskan crab braised fork-tender in wine and butter. The fried fish is always crisp; the broiled fish, always moist; and the steamed fish dinners are much appreciated by dieters. To these add copious salads served in soufflé dishes and homemade sherbets and ice cream (caffein addicts will swoon over the coffee flavor) and you'll understand the Berkowitz success.

Success has its drawbacks, however, and among them are the long lines, as Legal refuses to accept reservations. (Apply for a Legal credit card next time you're there as it will help you to be seated faster.) The house has two other quirky policies: you pay when you order and you receive your food as soon as it is cooked, not necessarily the moment your companions receive theirs. (The former can be remedied by requesting an open tab.) The high noise levels make Legal Sea Foods a dubious choice for intimate dining, but honeymooners may wish to order the caviar special, an ounce of beluga and a bottle of 1973 Dom Perignon for $87.95. And speaking of wine, the Berkowitzes have an excellent stock of California boutique vintages. Make your selection from the ream of computer print-outs that serve as a list.

THE MASS. BAY CO.

Rating: ★★★

Type of cuisine: seafood

Price range: appetizers from $3.50–5.50; entrees $8.50–17.50

39 Dalton St. (the Sheraton-Boston Hotel), Boston

Telephone: 236–2000

Hours: open seven days a week from 11:30 a.m.–10:30 p.m. (lunch served from 11:30 a.m.–2:30 p.m.; dinner from 5:30–10:30 p.m.)

Reservations recommended

Major credit cards accepted

Full bar

Wheelchair access adequate

Dress: jacket and tie or turtleneck

This classy fish house may be one of the best kept restaurant secrets in town. Where else can you get such local delicacies as bluefish, swordfish and mako shark grilled over mesquite wood, a scrubby Texas tree that has become the *ne plus ultra* of barbecuing? The Mass. Bay Co. serves a first-rate *ceviche* (uncooked seafood marinated with chili and lime juice) and the clam chowder (loaded with bacon and leeks) took first place at the Boston Chowderfest. But one of the best things of all about the Mass. Bay Co. is that, even on weekends, it accepts reservations!

Oysters? The Company's clams and oysters come on fish-shaped platters with tiny bottles of Tabasco sauce and lemons wrapped with seed-stopping cheesecloth. How about smoked fish? The Mass. Bay Co. smokes salmon and trout on the premises and serves both with a picture-pretty entourage of scallion brushes and radish carnations. Other entrees range from homemade pasta garnished with shellfish (sometimes a trifle overcooked) to crumb-topped scrod and boiled or baked lobster. All main courses are accompanied by moist, French-fried spiral potatoes. The tasty steamers are mercifully free of sand.

Desserts at the Company include a refreshingly tart cranberry-raisin confection called "Brant's pie" and a number of innovative sundaes such as the remarkable banana-nirvana sauce. A small but well-chosen wine list features vintages from France, California and the Pacific Northwest.

As for decor, the split-level dining room is highlighted by blue and white awnings, a wall-sized photograph of Boston Harbor back in the days of the great sailing ships, and indolent ceiling fans that twirl beneath a wire cage ceiling. The tables are well-spaced and booths are separated by ultrasuede partitions.

NEWBURY STEAK HOUSE

Rating: ★★

Type of cuisine: meat and potatoes

Price range: entrees $6.00–11.00 (salad bar included)

94 Mass. Ave., Boston

Telephone: 536–0184

Hours: open seven days a week from noon–midnight

Reservations accepted, but not usually necessary

Major credit cards accepted

Full bar

Wheelchair access fair

Dress: nice casual

I wish I could tell you about the breadth of the menu or the nature of the daily specials at the Newbury Steak House. The truth is, whenever I go to this Back Bay steak house, I always order one of two items: the prime rib or the London broil. The former is a generous, well-marbled slab of roast beef served with *jus* and a baked potato. The latter features a full-sized dinner plate carpeted with blood-rare, well-charred, paper-thin steak slices served with mushroom gravy and crunchy sautéed onions.

The beef is not the only charm of the Newbury Steak House; the freshly baked, country-style white bread served with dinner is as light and moist a loaf as you'll find anywhere. The price of an entree also gains you access to a salad bar stocked with peppers, garbanzo beans, better than average tomatoes, and iceberg lettuce. The French fries taste previously frozen but you can't go wrong with a baked potato and sour cream. Why, there is even a plate of free brownies by the antique brass cash register in the unlikely event you should feel hungry after a dessert of fudgy chocolate cake or Rowinsky's cheesecake.

The "Wild West" is alive and well at this neighborhood haunt with its massive ceiling beams, Tiffany-style lamps, and wooden Indian standing guard at the entryway. And this is one steak house where you can enjoy the privacy of wooden booths and tables draped with red checkered cloths without the din of children careening off the walls as you would find at similar restaurants in the suburbs. (No one seems to have kids in

Back Bay!) Other house specialties include broiled bluefish and scrod and well-charred burgers. Then again, it's nice to know you can always depend on the prime rib and London broil.

PEASANT STOCK

Rating: ★★

Type of cuisine: peasant

Price range: appetizers from $2.00–4.00; entrees $8.00–12.00

421 Washington St., Somerville

Telephone: 354–9528

Hours: open for lunch Tuesday–Friday from noon–2 p.m.; for dinner Monday–Saturday from 6–10 p.m.; and for Sunday brunch from noon–2 p.m.

Reservations recommended for music events; seats in the main dining room on a first-come-first-serve basis

No credit cards, but personal checks accepted

Wine and beer

Wheelchair access adequate

Entertainment: live chamber music, singing, and theater Monday–Thursday

Dress: sportscoat and tie to casual

"If music be the food of love, play on," sighed Duke Orsino in *Twelfth Night*. The Peasant Stock Restaurant has it all—good food, fine music, and even a touch of romance—in a setting that is as relaxed and comfortable as eating at home.

The Peasant Stock was founded in 1970 by Tesair Lauve, a harpsichordist who performs regularly at the restaurant, and Jerry Pierce, a one-time divinity student whose love of song was as powerful as his impatience with graduate school.

Two years after the Peasant Stock's opening, the couple launched their musical evenings program featuring classical chamber music, Gay

Nineties drinking songs, and everything in between. Dinner in the music room is served from 7–8:30 with dessert and wine to be enjoyed during the entertainment. The Sunday brunch theater features plays by local and national playwrights, and special banquets, like the recent "Schubertiade," are held to honor famous composers' birthdays.

But to visit the Peasant Stock for the music alone would be to overlook an estimable cuisine prepared by Pierce and his Orleans-born cooks. The menu changes daily and features such robust international fare as Argentine beef stew, pasta with squid and garlic, chicken stuffed with ricotta cheese and prosciutto, and Idaho trout with scallion butter and cucumbers. Dessert could include a praline cake with bourbon buttercream or a honey mousse created in honor of Saint Patrick's day. Also praiseworthy is the restaurant's practice of giving another chef credit on the menu when his recipe is used.

The decor of the Peasant Stock is best described as "funky," with mismatched but comfortable chairs surrounding tables faced with hand-painted tiles. The main dining room, which seats 40, boasts a Bruegel-esque painting of a gargantuan nude sprawled atop a banquet table. Access to the dining area is gained through the Peasant Stock wine bar, one of the few in Cambridge. The service and mood of the restaurant are as informal as the setting.

LA PRIMAVERA

Rating: ★★★

Type of cuisine: Northern Italian

Price range: appetizers from $3.50–6.00; entrees $12.00–16.00

50 Church St., Cambridge

Telephone: 491–3735

Hours: open for lunch Monday–Friday from 11:30 a.m.–2:30 p.m.; for dinner daily from 5–10 p.m.; Sunday brunch from 10:30 a.m.–3 p.m.

Reservations recommended

Major credit cards accepted

Full bar

Wheelchair access adequate

Dress: jacket and tie or turtleneck

Is Harvard Square about to become Boston's newest Italian quarter? This student center has long had the area's highest concentration of pizza parlors but the founding of Upstairs at the Pudding (see p. 31) has finally brought serious Italian cooking to Cambridge. And now comes a new Italian restaurant, La Primavera, located on the site of the late Rufus Porter in the basement of the Atrium on Church St.

This stylish restaurant specializes in the cooking of Northern Italy, a cuisine popular with young American chefs for the subtlety of its flavors. CIA (Culinary Institute of America)-trained chef, Jay Trubee, uses such fashionable ingredients as pink peppercorns, raspberry vinegar, and sun-dried tomatoes to create his *insalata de misticanza* (fennel, radish, and celeriac salad), *tagliatelle con porri* (ribbon-thin noodles with leek sauce), and *crispelli fiorentina* (crepes filled with ricotta cheese and fragrant mortadella sausage). His moist, crusty Tuscan bread, served with a complimentary *tapanade* (tangy olive-anchovy dip), sets a new standard for restaurant breadbaskets. A daily changing dessert tray proposes such temptations as kahlua-laced chocolate mousse and rum-soaked ladyfingers sandwiched with ricotta cheese and whipped cream.

La Primavera is a pretty restaurant, its chandeliers and mirrored walls compensating for the sense of claustrophobia one often feels in basement restaurants. The well-spaced tables are covered with snowy cloths, flanked by bow-back Windsor chairs, and crowned with solitary tulips. The courtyard, faced with brick, tile, and flower boxes, makes an ideal spot for alfresco dining. The Sunday brunch provides an Italian switch on Continental classics featuring eggs Benedictine made with *pancetta* (dry-cured Italian bacon) and "Italian" toast flavored with cinnamon and sambucca.

SABATINO'S

Rating: ★★½

Type of cuisine: Italian

Price range: appetizers from $1.00–5.00; entrees $5.00–11.00

14 Parmenter St., Boston

Telephone: 367–1504

Hours: open Tuesday–Saturday from 11 a.m.–10 p.m.

Reservations accepted for parties of 4 or more

Major credit cards accepted

Beer and wine

Wheelchair access good

Dress: nice casual

Boston restaurant goers may be surprised to find few North End dining establishments in this guide book. After all, isn't Boston's Italian quarter the area's largest ethnic neighborhood and aren't there more restaurants per square block here than anywhere else in town? Yes, there are a lot of Italian restaurants here but most of them smother their food under melted cheese, mountains of breadcrumbs, and oceans of tomato sauce. Among the few exceptions is an unpretentious and relatively obscure North End dining spot named for its Avelino-born chef, Billy Sabatino.

Sabatino's specializes in the sort of uncomplicated, delicate but filling food one would find at a *trattoria* in Italy. Here, the antipasto features prosciutto, sausage, provolone, and artichokes on a bed of lettuce and not, as is often the case, a salad topped with miserly snippets of cold cuts. And speaking of salad, the escarole soup, made with tangy escarole leaves which lose their bitterness when simmered in hardy broth, comes highly recommended. Sabatino's veal *saltimbocca* lives up to its name. It literally "jumps in the mouth," stuffed as it is with prosciutto and mozzarella, fried in a fluffy batter, and served with wine sauce. I also recommend the peppery lemon chicken and steak Sabatino, the latter smothered with fried onions. Desserts are rather limited. It would be best to finish your evening over cannoli and capuccino at the Caffe Paradiso (see p. 87) around the corner.

Located on a North End side street seldom visited by tourists, Sabatino's boasts a red-on-red interior popular with Italian restaurants. Its walls are faced with brick, its tables are draped with red cloths, and there is seating for 55. The hostess (Billy's niece) and many of the customers speak Italian, lending the restaurant further authenticity. As you might guess from the high degree of professionalism in the food and service, this is not Billy Sabatino's first restaurant. The short, personable chef worked at Boston's esteemed Ritz-Carlton and ran the popular Abruzzi restaurant before opening Sabatino's in August, 1981.

ST. BOTOLPH RESTAURANT

Rating: ★★★

Type of cuisine: nouvelle American/Continental

Price range: appetizers from $3.50–7.00; entrees $12.00–19.00

99 St. Botolph Street, Boston

Telephone: 266–3030

Hours: open for lunch Monday–Friday from 12–2:30 p.m.; for dinner Sunday–Thursday from 6–10:30 p.m., Friday and Saturday till midnight; Saturday and Sunday brunch from 11 a.m.–3 p.m.; light suppers and dessert served in the café Monday–Friday from 3 p.m.–midnight, Saturday and Sunday from 6 p.m.–midnight

Reservations recommended

Major credit cards accepted

Full bar

Wheelchair access poor

Dress: jacket and tie or turtleneck

The original Botolph, patron saint of Boston, was a 6th century missionary who founded a town in northeast England. (By the process of elision "St. Botolph's Town" became "Boston.") There is nothing monastic about Boston's St. Botolph, a fashionable bar and restaurant that opened in a restored, nineteenth century South End townhouse in 1975. The Boston "saint" is recognizable by its ornate brickwork and superb corner turret. (Request a seat by its curved windows.) The stylish interior with its brick walls, overhead spotlights, Breuer-style chairs, and sunny windows has no doubt served as the model for a subsequent generation of townhouse restaurants.

The food at St. Botolph might best be described as "nouvelle American," blending French, Italian, and Greek cooking techniques into a forthright cuisine for the 80's. Baked oysters come with a topping of bell peppers and Portuguese sausage; a velvety split pea soup with tangy shreds of prosciutto. A tuna steak (fresh tuna tastes almost like beef when grilled) wears a brie cheese-scallion sauce, while lamb receives the unexpected enhancement of French goat cheese and mustard. Daily specials include two fish dishes (the St. Botolph menu leans heavily toward seafood) while vegetables are prepared simply to retain their garden freshness. The dessert offerings seem expressly ordained for the chocoholic but if you don't care for silky chocolate mousse cake or a whipped cream-laced chocolate cashew torte, there is always hot walnut pie or raspberry sherbet with Cointreau to satisfy your craving for sugar.

When the weather is good St. Botolph makes a lovely brunch spot; the sun streams through the windows of the massive turret as you savor a crusty camembert cheese *en croûte* or perhaps eggs St. Botolph garnished with steak and béarnaise sauce. Light suppers are served in the cafe until midnight and the lounge attracts a well-heeled, South End clientele. The restaurant is no bargain but most customers feel that they get their money's worth.

SCOTCH 'N SIRLOIN

Rating: ★★

Type of cuisine: meat and potatoes

Price range: appetizers $3.00–5.00; entrees $7.00–15.00

77 North Washington St., Boston

Telephone: 723–3677

Hours: open for dinner Monday–Thursday from 5:30–10:30 p.m.; Friday–Sunday till 11:30 p.m.; lounge open on the weekends till 2 a.m.

Reservations recommended

Major credit cards accepted

Full bar

Wheelchair access adequate

Entertainment: live entertainment nightly (dancing to golden oldies on Fridays)

Dress: jacket and tie or turtleneck

Admen will tell you that what counts in the restaurant business is not the steak but the sizzle. Boston's Scotch 'N Sirloin, one of nine in a North American chain, has sizzle aplenty and its meats and seafood are as good as most in town.

First the sizzle. Guests ride a freight elevator to the 8th floor of a renovated North End warehouse. The walls and high, barrel-vaulted ceiling are brick, the former decorated with antique handtools, the latter with dangling, bare light bulbs. Huge picture windows, garlanded with hanging ferns, offer an impressive view of downtown. The cocktail waitresses, leggy ladies in leotards, serve spicy bloody Marys in glasses the size of flower vases. The busboys clad with leather aprons, fill the water glasses from pewter pitchers.

True to the sell-the-sizzle format, the Scotch menu is printed on a workman's lunchbox. Steaks come in all sizes, from petit prime rib (well-marbled) to nicely charred filet mignons and sirloins, the latter available in combination with crab, shrimp, and lobster. Clams and oysters on the half shell and shrimp cocktail are sold à la carte as are vegetable side dishes which include sautéed mushrooms and broccoli. Both seem superfluous after a trip to the salad bar (included with the price of dinner), a well-stocked assortment of romaine as well as crisp head lettuce, raw vegetables, alfalfa sprouts, and garlicky Caesar-style dressing, the ensemble marred only by the insult of store-bought croutons. The lemon cream pie is all fluff and whipped cream (and too much bitter lemon rind) but the hot fudge sundae is the sort of dish I wake up thinking about in the middle of the night.

The Scotch is a popular restaurant so reservations, particularly on days of sporting events at the nearby Boston Garden, are a must. Nightly entertainment in the spacious lounge includes live music and dancing to golden oldies on Fridays. Would that the service in the dining room was as lively as the leg work on the dance floor! Expect a 20-minute wait to get into the lounge on the weekends.

SEVENTH INN

Rating: ★★½

Type of cuisine: health food

Price range: entrees at dinner $6.00–10.00

272 Newbury St., Boston

Telephone: 247–2475

Hours: open Monday–Wednesday for lunch from 11:30 a.m.–5 p.m. and for dinner from 5 p.m.–9 p.m.; Thursday–Saturday till 10 p.m.

Reservations accepted

Major credit cards accepted

BYOB

Wheelchair access poor

Dress: casual

Restaurants may change their menus, do change their chefs, and not infrequently change their locations. But the hardest thing for a restaurant to change is its reputation. Hiroshi Hayashi, former chef and current owner of the Seventh Inn restaurant, has learned this truth the hard way. Hayashi purchased the Seventh Inn from macrobiotics patriarch Michio Kushi in the summer of 1981 and, although he has broken with the health food hard line, he is still trying to convince the public that non-macrobiotics will find much here to their liking.

The Seventh Inn has long been one of my favorite restaurants, specializing in seafood dishes and international vegetarian classics. You can begin your meal with Middle East *hoomis* (chickpea dip) or some good old Yankee cornbread, savoring a main course of Japanese *tempura* (batter-fried vegetables) or pasta with Italian cheese. The backbone of the menu is formed by such health food classics as *bancha* (Japanese twig) tea, *miso* soup, salad with *tahini* (sesame seed paste) dressing, and a vegetarian platter featuring a soup, green, grain, and vegetable *du jour*. But to my thinking, the star attractions of the Seventh Inn are the daily fish specials which include smoked trout, mussels steamed in wine, salmon broiled with ginger-tamari sauce, or scrod (a trifle undercooked) topped with anchovies, herbs, and shallots. As you would expect at a health food restaurant, vegetables are briefly steamed to retain their crispness and vitamins. The maple syrup-sweetened desserts, like pecan pie and delectable pear crunch, prove that fine pastries *can* be made without sugar.

In the fall of 1982 the Seventh Inn moved from its sprawling Park Square storefront to a cozy basement on Newbury St. The new location boasts white brick walls, hanging greenery, and homey wooden tables graced with fresh flowers and illuminated by recessed lighting. At the rear of the dining room, a squadron of white-capped chefs bustle around a huge, open kitchen. (Budding chefs may be interested to know that the Seventh Inn has one of Boston's few chef apprenticeship programs.) In this salubrious setting, serenaded by Keith Jarret music, the solitary diner will feel as comfortable as members of larger parties. The restaurant does a lively carry-out business, too.

SOL AZTECA

Rating: ★★★

Type of cuisine: Mexican

Price range: appetizers from $2.00–4.25; entrees $8.50–13.00

914 A Beacon St., Boston

Telephone: 262–0909

Hours: open for dinner Monday–Thursday from 6–10:30 p.m.; Friday and Saturday from 5:30–11 p.m.; and Sunday from 5–10 p.m.

No reservations after 6 p.m.

Major credit cards accepted

Beer and wine

Wheelchair access poor

Entertainment: live guitar music every Monday and Tuesday

Dress: nice casual

The street cooking of Mexico, with its variations on a stuffed tortilla theme, is well known to North America. Less familiar is Mexican haute cuisine which varies boldly from region to region and is as elaborate as anything from Central Europe or the Szechuan province of China. At this writing, Boston lacks a great cheap Mexican restaurant but if you are willing to spend $15 or so, you can have excellent highbrow Mexican fare at the Sol Azteca, located near the border of Boston and Brookline. Sol Azteca ranks among those rare restaurants that have managed to survive numerous rave reviews and a subsequent dining room expansion without a serious deterioration in the cooking. Meals begin with complimentary *salsa* and chips, the former loaded with fresh *cilantro* (coriander leaves), the latter made from crisply fried tortillas. Appetizers range from familiar *queso asado* (cheese broiled with spicy chorizo sausage) to exotic *higaditos mexicanos* (chicken livers in tomato sauce) and *nopalitos* (tangy cactus salad). But delicious as these are, I suggest you skip them, unless you have the appetite of an ox, as the entrees here are almost large enough to serve two.

My favorite dish is the *puerco en adobo*, pounded pork tenderloin marinated with orange juice and smoky *chipotle* chili peppers (the latter smoked over banana leaf fires). This fiery fare is also available as an appetizer called *carnitas* and the merest mouthful of either tastes like a bite of a high voltage cable! The most historic dish at the Sol Azteca is the *mole poblano*, chicken with fiery "chocolate" sauce, a throwback to pre-Colonial days when the Aztecs added unsweetened chocolate to their chili sauce for extra richness and a hint of bitterness. Not all the food at the Sol Azteca is incendiary and milder items include *enchilades verdes* (soft tortillas filled with chicken and green tomato sauce, topped with sour cream) and *chiles rellenos* (spicy green peppers filled with cheese and fried in batter). Entrees come attractively garnished with fluffy rice, crunchy marinated cabbage, and the meatiest refried beans in town.

The copious portions of the entrees make dessert a matter of overkill, but do save room for the *plantanos con cajeta* (neatly fanned banana slices topped with ultra-rich Mexican caramel sauce). Traditionally *cajeta* is made with goat's milk—the Sol's version might aptly be described as a sundae without the ice cream. The cinnamon-scented *sangria* here is mercifully free of the sugary cloy found in most fruit-wine punches and the *cafe de olla* (coffee with chocolate and cinnamon) brings the meal to a delectable close.

The colorful decor of Sol Azteca makes you forget that you are dining in a basement. The tables are made of hand-painted tiles; the walls are decorated with wrought iron, Indian blankets, and other Mexican handicrafts. Even the waiters wear gaily embroidered peasant shirts. All are prompt but some are less polite than others. Non-smokers will appreciate the segregation of dining rooms and everyone enjoys the music provided by a guitar duo two nights a week.

SOL POSTO (THE SUNSET CAFE)

Rating: ★★

Type of cuisine: Iberian

Price range: appetizers from $3.75–4.50; entrees $6.00–12.00

851 Cambridge St., Cambridge

Telephone: 547–2938

Hours: open Monday–Thursday from 11 a.m.–11 p.m.; Friday and Saturday till midnight; Sunday from noon–11 p.m.

Reservations accepted, but necessary only on the weekend

Major credit cards accepted

Full bar

Wheelchair access adequate

Entertainment: Portuguese folk music on Saturday

Dress: casual

It's 9 p.m. and already the customers are singing. Welcome to the Sol Posto (known in English as the Sunset Café), a popular Portuguese restaurant in the heart of "Little Lisbon" in Cambridge.

Dinner begins with complimentary olives and tangy Portuguese pickled cauliflower. The *caldo verde* (olive oil-laced kale soup) is good, the *meijoas a espagnhola* (spicy Spanish-style clams) are better, but whatever you do, don't miss the *chourico flameado* (peppery Portuguese sausage doused with flaming brandy). Entrees range from *carne a alentejana* (pork with littlenecks) to *polvo com molho verde* (octopus in a redolent sauce of wine, herbs, and garlic). Perhaps you'll be lucky enough to arrive on a night when *lulas grelhadas* or *cabrito assado* are the daily specials: the former is marinated, grilled squid and the latter, roast goat (it tastes like a cross between pork and veal). Both are delicious.

The Sol's box-like dining room boasts red carpets, red tablecloths, plywood wainscoting, and white stucco arches. The service can be slow and dessert is generally not worth waiting for. The entrance on the left leads to the restaurant; the one on the right, to a boisterous neighborhood bar. You hear lots of Portuguese here which speaks highly for the Sol's authenticity.

TATSUKICHI-BOSTON

Rating: ★★★

Type of cuisine: Japanese

Price range: appetizers from $1.50–5.00; entrees $6.00–11.00

189 State St., Boston

Telephone: 720–2468

Hours: open for lunch Monday–Saturday from 11:30 a.m.–3 p.m.; for dinner from 5–10 p.m.

Reservations accepted; recommended for private dining rooms

Major credit cards accepted

Full bar

Wheelchair access difficult

Dress: nice casual to jacket and tie

This Quincy Market area restaurant features the exposed brick, sturdy butcher block, and hanging plants of a typical downtown fern bar, but make no mistake, Tatsukichi-Boston is authentically Japanese. So authentic, in fact, that its extensive menu lists many dishes I have never seen at other Boston Japanese restaurants. Not everyone will wax grandiloquent about *ikura-orashi* (salmon caviar with musty Japanese radish) or *hiya-yakko* (bean curd with pickled ginger and scallion served in a bowl of ice water) but even a finicky eater would enjoy the *kushiagi* (bamboo skewers threaded with such delicacies as scallops with green beans and pork with fresh pineapple, crisply fried in batter).

Sushi fans will find here no fewer than 37 different kinds of raw fish-vinegared rice cakes ranging from innocuous *tatsukichi-maki* (avocado and king crab roll) to exotic *tobiko* (flying fish egg) and sweet, omelette-like *tomago*. Both the sushi and sashimi (uncooked fish served with soy sauce and spicy Japanese horseradish) are stunningly presented with *gari* (pickled ginger) to refresh your palate. Other house specialties include *hourenso-gomaae* (cold cooked spinach with black sesame seed dressing), *teriyaki* (beef, chicken, or fish broiled with a sweet-salty sauce), and *agar agar* (a jello-like seaweed extract served with fruit for dessert).

Opened in January, 1981, by a Japanese and an American who became fast friends at the Boston University Business School,

Tatsukichi-Boston occupies three floors of the red brick Foreign Affairs building at the foot of State St. The main dining room has both Western-style tables and booths for purists who wish to sit cross-legged. Upstairs, there is a traditional *karaoke* (Japanese "bottle" club) where regular customers, mostly Japanese business men, buy and store their drinks by the bottle. The Foreign Affairs lounge in the basement serves Japanese and American snacks amid wicker chairs and live piano music.

THAI CUISINE

Rating: ★★½

Type of cuisine: Thai

Price range: appetizers from $2.00–4.00; entrees $6.50–12.00

14A Westland Street, Boston

Telephone: 262–1485

Hours: open for lunch from 11:30 a.m.–3 p.m.; for dinner from 5–10:30 p.m.; seven days a week

No reservations

Major credit cards accepted

Beer and wine

Wheelchair access good

Dress: casual

Hot-food fans rued the closing of Boca Loca, a small, funky Mexican storefront restaurant in back of Symphony Hall. But no matter, the location has now been appropriately filled by Thai Cuisine, a restaurant that serves equally spicy food at equally affordable prices. The similarity between the name and menu of Thai Cuisine and that of Boston's oldest Thai restaurant, Bangkok Cuisine, is no accident; the newcomer was opened by the former chef of the latter.

A dinner at Thai Cuisine begins with a bowl of *shrimp chips* (the Asian version of cheese doodles) which look like scraps of styrofoam and dissolve on your tongue like snowflakes. For appetizers order the *sate,* char-broiled beef kebabs served with cucumber-chili sauce, and avoid the *tod man pla*, fried bluefish patties, which are rubbery and greasy. I also recommend the rich chicken-coconut soup and *kang liang* (shrimp soup laced with miniature corn ears, fresh basil leaves and tongue-searing blasts of pepper).

My favorite dish here is *yum koon csiang*, a cold, sweet-spicy salad of onions, cucumbers and Chinese sausage (the last ingredient is as sweet as Smithfield ham). I also like the *gai pud gra prao*, a pyromaniacal orgy of chicken, onion, pineapple, basil and peppers. *Pla pae ca* (bass steamed with ginger and scallions) is a milder dish and easy to eat, too, because the fish is boned before steaming. The *pad thai* (stir-fried noodles with shrimp and vegetables) is also pleasant. Be sure to ask for the condiment tray so that you can sprinkle grated peanuts and pickled chilis on your noodles.

Thai Cuisine has a simple dining room. The tan and brown walls are appointed with Asian artifacts and sconces and high ceilings help cut down on the noise. Liquid refreshments run from hopsy Thai beer to saccharin Thai iced coffee. Thai Cuisine provides spoons and forks but no knives or chopsticks, because in Thailand knives are most commonly used for killing people and so are thought to bring bad luck to a dinner table. As at the Bangkok, Thai Cuisine's 50 seats are insufficient to meet the demands of an enthusiastic public.

TIGERLILIES

Rating: ★★

Type of cuisine: contemporary

Price range: appetizers from $1.50–5.00; entrees $8.00–14.00

23 Joy St., Boston

Telephone: 523–0609

Hours: open for lunch Sunday–Friday from 11:30 a.m.–3:30 p.m.; for dinner Sunday–Thursday from 5–10 p.m., and Friday and Saturday till 11 p.m.; Sunday brunch from 11:30 a.m.–3:30 p.m.

Reservations recommended

Major credit cards accepted

Beer and wine

Wheelchair access tricky

Dress: nice casual to jacket and tie

This pretty restaurant may be a newcomer to historic Beacon Hill, but its basement dining rooms and shady courtyard reflect the splendor of a bygone era. The dining rooms boast timbered ceilings, white brick walls hung with prints of flowers, and manorial fireplaces perennially ablaze with embers. The courtyard, paved with brick and decorated with flower beds and a reflecting pool fed by a bronze dolphin fountain, affords an oasis of calm amid the bustle of urban Boston.

Opened by stockbroker-turned-restaurateur Joann Crawford, Tigerlilies serves a contemporary cuisine at surprisingly reasonable prices. Soups, like the cream of cauliflower or cabbage soup laced with Pernod, are simmered from scratch and salads, like the tuna and anchovy-enriched niçoise, are copious and refreshing. Entrees range from better than average sautéed chicken livers served on a split croissant to occasional dishes of gastronomic pretention, like the *harlequin terrine* (a colorful mosaic of chicken mousse and vegetables) or salmon with mustard sauce broiled to a leopard skin mottle. Vegetables retain their pristine crunch (sometimes too much so). The *crème brulée* (custard with a hard, caramelized sugar crust) would bring any meal to a memorable close.

Tigerlilies draws lunchtime crowds of State House officials and local executives. The service is friendly though a trifle amateurish. After an arduous struggle with its staid Beacon Hill neighbors, Tigerlilies finally acquired a wine license and, in general, the wine prices are as reasonable as those of the food. Parking on Beacon Hill can be difficult. I suggest you park in one of the lots on Cambridge Street and walk up gas-lit Joy Street.

29 NEWBURY ST.

Rating: ★★★½

Type of cuisine: nouvelle cuisine/contemporary

Price range: appetizers $2.50–6.00; entrees $5.00–15.00

29 Newbury St., Boston

Telephone: 536–5137

Hours: open seven days a week from 11:30 a.m.–1 a.m. (lunch served 11:30 a.m.; dinner till 12:30 a.m.; light fare till 1 a.m.)

Reservations recommended (request a booth)

Major credit cards accepted

Full bar

Wheelchair access tricky

Dress: nice casual

1981 was a tough year for Back Bay restaurant goers. In November, 1981 they lost C'Est Si Bon, an elegant French restaurant with a bay window overlooking the Boston Garden. A few months earlier, the English Tea Room closed its doors after decades of purveying economical fare to its neighbors. Every cloud has its silver lining, however, and the disappointed patrons of the aforementioned establishments were more than amply consoled by the opening of 29 Newbury St., a chic and surprisingly reasonably priced restaurant run by former C'Est Si Bon owner, John Aumont, in the Newbury St. basement once occupied by the English Tea Room.

This fashionable restaurant serves an international menu prepared by a gifted, young chef named Kenneth Lyons, who seems determined to prove that *nouvelle cuisine* is alive and well in Boston. The house salads, served on the oversized plates that have become the calling cards of the "new cooking," feature such exotic ingredients as lamb's lettuce, *radicchio* (a red leaf lettuce in the chicory family), sun-dried tomatoes, and goat cheese dressing. Duck breasts are cooked and served rare like steak, accompanied by daily changing sauces that might include raspberries and raspberry vinegar. Fish fillets are pounded as thin as poker chips, sautéed for mere seconds, and topped with caviar to make another 29 Newbury St. specialty, salmon flip-flop. Not all the fare is fancy here; you can also order a well-charred burger or Scandinavian open-faced sand-wiches on the terrace. Ice creams and sherbets are homemade as is the *pot de crème* tart, one of the richest, moistest chocolate desserts I have ever tasted.

Twenty Nine Newbury St. doesn't feel like a basement restaurant. Its rectangular dining room is brightened with peach-colored grass cloth and the tables and booths are draped with snowy linens and graced with freshly cut flowers and lamplight. The bar area, with its handsome green marble tables, makes a stylish place to watch passersby on Newbury St. while sipping the house cocktail, a Pimm's cup garnished with a refresh-ing slice of cucumber. Waiters and waitresses sport New Wave haircuts and serve light fare on the sidewalk terrace and a late-night menu to theater-goers. The menu remains the same throughout the day making 29 Newbury St. a potentially pricey place for lunch but an equally potentially reasonable spot for dinner.

THE BUDGET GOURMET

Boston's Best Cheap Eats

AEGEAN FARE

Rating: ★

Type of cuisine: Greek

Price range: entrees from $4.00–7.00

739 Commonwealth Ave., Boston

Telephone: 267–2202

Hours: open Monday–Friday from 7 a.m.–4 a.m.; Saturday and Sunday
   8 a.m.–4 a.m.

No reservations

Major credit cards accepted

Full bar

Wheelchair access good

Dress: casual

This cavernous Greek restaurant stands in the heart of the Kenmore
Square disco district. To judge from its gaudy decor, Saturday night fever
is catching. The Aegean Fare may be Boston's only Greek restaurant
decorated with neon signs, huge arched canopies, hanging plants, glim-
mering mirrors, and butcher block tables. But the popularity of the
Aegean Fare is due as much to its late hours, low prices, and copious
portions as to the eye-catching interior.

   The menu lists 45 Greek specialties plus another 50 American deli
items ranging from hamburgers to knishes. Like most restaurants, the
Aegean Fare does its best job with appetizers which run from a simple
plate of Greek olives and *feta* (brine-cured, sheep's milk cheese) to

spanakopita (spinach-cheese "pie" made with infinitesimally thin sheets of filo dough). The chefs' fondness for garlic can be seen in such traditional Greek dips as *satziki* (yogurt-cucumber dip), *skorthalia* (mashed potatoes with garlic and vinegar), and *taramosalata* (caviar spread). All three are served with pita bread for dipping. Given such an embarrassment of riches, the only wise thing to do is to order a *pikilia* (appetizer sampler) which includes fresh cucumbers, stuffed grape leaves (I prefer the Armenian-style grape leaves sold at the Eastern Lamejun Company in Belmont, however), and rounds of sweet Greek sausage in addition to the items mentioned above.

Aegean Fare casseroles, like the *moussaka* (eggplant with ground beef and bechamel sauce), have a steam table heaviness that leaves you better off ordering grilled fare, like *souvlaki* (lamb shish kebab) or *gyro* (as in our word "gyroscope"—ground lamb and beef roasted on a vertical spit). The restaurant also excels in the sort of sugary, syrup-soaked desserts that make Near East pastries so popular with sweet lovers and include *baklava* (ground nuts sandwiched between layers of buttery filo dough), *kopenhai* (syrup-soaked cake sandwiched between layers of filo), and *kataifi* (a pastry that resembles shredded wheat). With dinner, order a bottle of retsina (resinated Greek wine) and with dessert, Greek coffee, which is made by boiling the grounds directly in the water. (Don't take the last sip!)

ALGIERS COFFEE HOUSE

Rating: ★★

Type of cuisine: international coffees and other beverages/Middle East and international snacks and pastries

Price range: cheap

40 Brattle St., Cambridge

Telephone: 492–1557

Hours: seven days a week from 10 a.m.–midnight

No reservations

No credit cards

No liquor

Wheelchair access poor

Entertainment: impromptu guitar concerts, but no regularly scheduled
program

Dress: casual

I have often wondered how the Algiers stays in business. The average
customer orders a single cup of coffee or tea and spends the next two hours
sipping it over a book (preferably by Kant or Marcuse) or a newspaper (*Le
Monde* or the New York Review of Books) or in heated discussion about
politics. Like a *café* in Paris, the price of a single beverage buys you a seat
for the afternoon. But unique to the Algiers is an international drink
menu that simultaneously boasts Viennese coffee with whipped cream,
Italian sodas, and mint tea from North Africa besides the usual espresso.

Opened in 1971 by Palestine-born Emile Durzi, the Algiers is one of
Harvard Square's most venerable coffee houses, drawing a cosmopolitan
clientele that is as apt to be speaking French or Arabic as well as English.

Gleaming brass *ibrikis* (hourglass-shaped pots used for making silty
Arabic coffee) hang above a massive Italian espresso machine on which
milk is foamed to make some of the frothiest *cappucino* (espresso topped
with clouds of steamed milk) in Boston. The Algiers is one of the few
places left that makes lemonade from scratch and where else can you
order such delicious iced beverages as espresso frappé and *orzata* (almond
extract, milk, and soda water)? But liquid refreshment is only half the
story because the Algiers serves excellent *hoomis* (chickpea dip), *tabbouli*
(cracked wheat salad), and other Middle East appetizers. The "meat pie,"
made with ground lamb, cracked wheat, and pine nuts, has a peppery
afterglow that will send you rushing for the side dish of mint-flavored
yogurt. Desserts are milder, fortunately, and range from syrupy baklava
(nut and filo dough pastry) to Western pecan pie and carrot cake.

A sunny, enclosed terrace has recently been added to the two
basement dining rooms (one for smokers, one for non-smokers) which
are decorated with colorful weavings and Middle East brass and lanterns.
Although there is no formally scheduled entertainment, impromptu
classical guitar concerts are frequently given by musicians who are
regular customers. In the summertime you can sip your coffee beneath a
grape trellis on a tiny outdoor terrace. You just might see a thin, bearded
fellow scribbling in a notebook: the Algiers is one of the rare restaurants
where this critic goes on his day off!

ANNAPURNA RESTAURANT

Rating: ★★½

Type of cuisine: Indian

Price range: appetizers from $1.20–2.95; entrees from $4.50–10.25

483 Cambridge Street, Worcester

Telephone: 755-7413

Hours: open for lunch Monday–Friday from 11:30 a.m.–2 p.m.; for dinner 7 days a week from 5–10 p.m.

Reservations accepted

No credit cards

BYOB

Wheelchair access adequate

Dress: casual

Annapurna is the name of a high peak in the Himalayas but the word also means "wholesome" or "complete" food in Sanskrit. There couldn't be a more appropriate name for this pleasant Worcester storefront specializing in the vegetarian cooking of the west coast Indian town of Udipi. Eastern food buffs will find here dishes relatively mild in seasoning but loaded with flavor, dishes rarely encountered at Indian restaurants in Boston. Carnivores will enjoy a menu so rich and varied they probably won't even notice the absence of meat.

Begin your meal with *masala* peanuts (cooked in spicy chickpea batter) or perhaps *samosa* (deep-fried vegetable patties) served with spicy *tamarind* (a tart fruit) sauce for dipping. Soups range from lemon *saru* (piping hot lentil broth) to *gunji* (a rice, lentil, and yogurt soup served chilled). The *bhojan* (complete dinners) include soup, appetizer, and a silver tray loaded with rice, vegetable curry, hot pickles, and *papad* (potato chip-like wafers made from lentils), not to mention the thickest, richest, creamiest yogurt I have ever tasted to help extinguish the fires. Everything is cooked to order with spicing adjusted to your taste. ("Hot" is relatively mild by Thai standards.) And what better way to end your meal than with such traditional Indian desserts as *gulab jamun* (pressed curds sprinkled with nuts and saffroned syrup) or, on special occasions, *malpoowa* (banana fritters doused with spices and raw sugar syrup)?

Unpretentious in its setting, Annapurna offers an attractive decor of Indian wall hangings, paisley tablecloths, tiled pillars, brass lamps, and twangy sitar music. The whirling fans are only partially effective in dispelling the heat of summer. Four times a year Annapurna stages 12- to 16-course banquets with dessert served at both the beginning and end of the meal. Among the more exotic specialties typically offered is *panaka*, a "tea" made with artichokes, tamarind, and honey. Call the restaurant, or send your address for the mailing list, for information on upcoming feasts.

B AND D DELI

Rating: ★★

Type of cuisine: breakfast/deli

Price range: cheap

1653B Beacon St., Brookline

Telephone: 566–9417

Hours: open Monday–Saturday from 5 a.m.–8 p.m., Sunday from 5 a.m.–3 p.m.

No reservations

No credit cards

Beer served

Wheelchair access good

Dress: casual

The B and D Deli may be the only greasy spoon in Boston that has a liquor license but this is only one of the restaurant's distinctions. The B and D also serves the most succulent corned beef and eggs in Brookline and butter-fried blintzes served with oceans of sour cream that Gargantua himself would be hard pressed to finish.

The B and D opens daily at five in the morning but late risers can sleep on assured that lunch here is as filling and tasty as breakfast. The *kreplach* (meat-filled dumplings that resemble won tons) are simmered in homemade chicken broth and the gefilte fish is prepared from scratch on the premises every Friday. Daily specials run from brisket to stuffed cabbage to a noodle *kugel* (a sweet noodle pudding) that's the size of a cobblestone.

This kosher-style luncheonette (decidedly not kosher, however, as ham is a house specialty) is not what you would call elegant, occupying a narrow Beacon St. storefront that is jammed with a handful of counter stools and small tables. Despite the close quarters, everyone shouts: the short-order cooks, the customers, and even the cashier at the exit. Expect a considerable wait for a table on weekend mornings.

BEETLE'S LUNCH

Rating: ★★

Type of cuisine: home-style breakfasts, lunches

Price range: cheap

120 Harvard Ave., Brighton

Telephone: 254–9457

Hours: open Tuesday–Friday from 8 a.m.–3:30 p.m.; Saturday from 9–3; Sunday from 10–3

No reservations

No credit cards

BYOB

Wheelchair access poor

Dress: casual

Punk rock and feminist vocals might not be everyone's idea of dinner music but few of the young clients who jam this New Wave luncheonette seem to mind the blaring sound system. The discord stops with the music, fortunately, because the Beetle puts out some of the best home-style cooking this side of the B and D Deli (see p. 79). The "Lunch" part of the restaurant's name tells only half the story because breakfast features freshly squeezed orange juice, French toast made with *challah* (Jewish egg bread), and hashbrowns topped with sour cream, the potatoes fried with their skins. Lunch tends to be vegetarian: spinach cheese pie, chili with homemade cornbread, and double crusted pizza rustica are typical specials. The popular Sunday brunch features eggs Benedict and *huevos rancheros*, the latter served on tortillas with spicy tomato sauce. Beetle owners Ellen Sperling and Laura Pattison do all their own baking on the premises and their banana-sour cream pie redefines the meaning of the word "decadence."

This tiny luncheonette has seven red stools at its counter, punky black-and-white floor tiles, and the stainless steel of a vintage diner. Feminist consciousness runs high here but men seem to be welcomed, too.

BEL CANTO

Rating: ★★

Type of cuisine: health food/Italian (pizza)

Price range: appetizers from $2.00–3.00; entrees $3.00–8.00

928 Mass. Ave., Cambridge

Telephone: 547–6120

253A Washington St., Somerville

Telephone: 623-5353

1715 Mass. Ave., Lexington

Telephone: 861-6556

Hours: open Sunday–Tuesday from 11 a.m.–10 p.m., Friday and Saturday till 11 p.m.

Carry-out available

No reservations

No credit cards

Full bar

Wheelchair access good

Dress: casual

Ever since the first Italian baker spread tomato sauce on leftover bread dough, a controversy has raged between people who like thin crust pizzas and those who favor deep-dish. I number among the latter, preferring most of all the chewy, deep-dish pizza the Sicilians call *torta*. This variety happens to be the specialty of a hippie-pizzeria-turned-respectable-restaurant-chain called Bel Canto.

The first Bel Canto occupied a tiny storefront, recently enlarged and renovated, on Mass. Ave. between Harvard and Central Squares. It was packed with a scruffy serving staff, less than immaculate tables, and customers who slaked their thirst from well-hidden brown paper bags. The counterculture trappings disappeared when Bel Canto moved to the suburbs. The Somerville and Lexington branches boast the exposed brick, polished red oak, and track lights shining on artsy photographs of any classy downtown fern bar. Brown-bagging has given way to bars with a full liquor license where you can savor sangria, frozen daiquiris, and bloody Marys that require both hands for holding.

Torta and *calzone* remain the house specialties. *Torta* is a thick-crusted pizza spread with tomato sauce or ricotta cheese sauce (my favorite) and piled high with broccoli and walnuts or pepperoni and homemade sausage. *Calzone* (the word means "underpants" in Italian) are pizza dough turnovers: my favorite is the *tradizionale* (filled with pepperoni, ricotta, and parmesan cheese) but I wouldn't turn my nose up at either the *lianata* (filled with garlic, olives, and anchovies) or the *tonno* (filled with tuna and spinach, the turnover shaped ingeniously like a fish). Both dishes are available with white flour or whole wheat crusts (I regard the latter as a Communist plot, but then again, I have never been much of a fan for health food).

Bel Canto salads make a meal in themselves, consisting of spinach, romaine lettuce, fresh mushrooms, and homemade croutons with nary a shred of iceberg lettuce or a tasteless cotton tomato. Appetizers range from some of the last homemade marinated mushrooms in Boston to "Martha's 5 O'Clocks," pizza dough triangles filled with mushrooms, onions, cumin seed and chili pepper. Desserts include carrot cake and a sophisticated ice cream concoction called "rum gousse."

The service may seem somewhat slower than that at most pizzerias; the *tortas* and *calzones*, however, are worth the wait.

BERTUCCI'S PIZZA AND BOCCE

Rating: ★★

Type of cuisine: pizza

Price range: cheap

197 Elm St., Somerville

Telephone: 776-9241

Hours: open Monday–Thursday from 11:30 a.m.–11 p.m.; Friday and Saturday till midnight; Sunday from 2–11 p.m.

Reservations recommended for large parties

No credit cards

BYOB

Wheelchair access manageable

Entertainment: bocce ball nightly

Dress: casual

For most of human history, excluding the last 100 years or so, bread has been baked in wood-fired ovens. I regard the advent of gas and electric stoves as a mixed blessing: cake and pastry baking is all but failproof these days but the quality of bread has suffered. Bertucci's Pizza and Bocce is perhaps the only bakery in greater Boston that still uses a wood-burning oven and until you've tasted their *panino* or *quatro stagione*, you haven't tasted pizza.

Bertucci's specializes in two things that are quintessentially Italian—pizza and bocce ball. The former, assembled on a marble workbench in the store window, includes a *quatro stagione* ("four seasons" pizza, topped with artichokes, peppers, mushrooms, and ham, one ingredient to a quadrant) and an unusual *panino* (pizza garnished with four cheeses instead of tomato sauce). Alternatively, you can try a *calzone* ("underpants," literally), a dough turnover filled with ham, cheese and ricotta. Both pizzas and calzones are baked on the floor of a massive brick oven stoked with fires of oak and maple. The embers are brushed to one side to make way for your pizza.

After dinner you can descend to the sand-lined alley in the basement of Bertucci's to play *bocce* (pronounced "bochi") ball, an Italian form of bowling. The first player tosses a tiny guide ball to the far end of the court.

The object of the game is to land your ball closest to the guide ball as well as knocking aside the spheres hurled by your opponents.

Located next to the original Steve's Ice Cream, this Davis Square pizzeria has a smart split-level decor of high tech lamps, gallery prints, and white walls trimmed with oak and brick. An airy atrium makes the basement bocce ball court visible from the upstairs dining area. Don't forget to bring a nice red wine for sipping with dinner.

"So who was Bertucci?" you ask. He was the Italian bricklayer who built the massive wood-fired oven.

BOB THE CHEF

Rating: ★★

Type of cuisine: soul food

Price range: entrees $4.00–6.00

604 Columbus Avenue, Boston

Telephone: 536–6204

Hours: open Tuesday–Saturday 11 a.m.–9 p.m.

No reservations

No credit cards

No liquor

Wheelchair access good

Dress: casual

Boston's Bob the Chef may well be the only soul food restaurant north of the Mason-Dixon line to have been honored by the visit of a United States president. Jimmy Carter stopped at this South End landmark in 1979. For 23 years Bob "the Chef" Morgan, who hails from Raleigh, North Carolina, has been packing 'em in for his smothered chicken, smoked ham hocks, black-eyed peas, buttery collard greens and barbecued spareribs—the latter so tender, the meat falls right off the bone.

Don't expect much in the way of atmosphere; this brightly lit luncheonette furnished with booths and formica tables has about as much character as a fast food joint. And above all, don't leave Bob the Chef without sampling the spice-scented sweet potato pie.

Bob, by the way, is the guy wearing a necktie under his chef's coat. His youthful demeanor belies his sixty-plus years.

BROOKLINE LUNCH

Rating: ★★

Type of cuisine: American/breakfast

Price range: cheap

9 Brookline St., Cambridge

Telephone: 354–9473

Hours: open Monday–Friday from 6:30 a.m.–6:30 p.m.; Saturday from 7 a.m.–2 p.m.

No reservations

No credit cards

No liquor

Wheelchair access poor

Dress: casual

For four decades this clean "greasy spoon" has provided its neighbors with matitudinal bliss in the form of homemade muffins, farm fresh "dropped" (poached) and sunny-side-up eggs, uncommonly thick ham slices, and bowls of favorite hot cereals. But breakfast is only half the story, because, as the name suggests, Brookline lunch does a lively noontime trade with its hardy soups, daily specials (roast beef hash served on Thursdays), and homemade rice, bread, and grapenut puddings. True, the man at the stove is a cook, not a chef, but that does not prevent his home-style food from being devoured with any less gusto.

The narrow storefront may be short on formal decor, but the atmosphere is as heady as the homemade navy bean soup. The ten stools at the counter and five worn wooden booths are in great demand among the loyal, largely blue collar, local following.

BUTECO

Rating: ★★★

Type of cuisine: Brazilian

Price range: appetizers from $0.75–2.00; entrees $5.75–8.00

130 Jersey St., Boston

Telephone: 247–9508

Hours: open for lunch Tuesday–Saturday from noon–4 p.m.; for dinner Tuesday–Sunday from 5:30–10 p.m.

Reservations recommended

No credit cards

Beer and wine

Wheelchair access tricky

Entertainment: live Latin jazz regularly but on no set schedule

Dress: casual

You can hear the Latin jazz well before you enter this restaurant. Buteco is Boston's premier Brazilian dining establishment, you see, and dinner here is as animated as a carnival in Rio!

Buteco, which translates roughly as "neighborhood joint" in Portuguese, was opened by Paolo Penna, a former photography student and transplanted Brazilian. To set the right mood, Paolo decorated the Fenway storefront with hanging plants, cable spool tables, and posters of his native Minas Gerais. A live jazz combo, often led by Paolo himself, fills the tiny restaurant with music. Reservations are advisable as the low prices draw budget-minded dinner guests in droves.

What does one order at an authentic Brazilian restaurant? Start with fried *manioc* (a starchy tuber also known as cassava) which tastes like a cross between potato and plantain and comes with spicy carrot sauce for dipping. Nor should you miss the hearts of palm salad garnished with the delicately flavored core of the palmetto plant and tossed with a tangy palm oil dressing.

House specialties include *frango cremoso* (marinated, grilled chicken breast with creamy mushroom sauce) and *picadinho* (beef stewed with onions and peppers and enough garlic to ward off legions of vampires). *Vapata* combines sole and shrimp in a spicy cream sauce while *espato* demonstrates how the Brazilians spice up shish kebab.

Buteco serves a dessert for every disposition, from a marble-smooth *flan* (caramel custard) for conservatives to *dolce con leche* (salty cheese with gooey, sweet caramel sauce) for adventurous eaters. As you would expect at a Latin restaurant, the strong, black coffee all but dissolves the spoon.

Buteco recently acquired a wine list and if you can overlook the right wing politics, the Argentinian Trappiche chardonnay makes an excellent wine for the money. Located near Fenway Park, Buteco is not a restaurant to drive to on the day of a ballgame.

CAFFE PARADISO

Rating: ★★

Type of cuisine: coffee/Italian pastries and ice cream/(Italian restaurant upstairs)

Price range: cheap (restaurant mid-priced)

255 Hanover St., Boston

Telephone: 523–8872

Hours: open Sunday–Thursday from 7 a.m.–midnight; Friday till 1 a.m.; Saturday till 2 a.m.

No reservations for the café

No credit cards for the café

Beer and wine

Wheelchair access fair

Dress: casual

This North End café is no stranger to the Italian-speaking old-timers, who linger here over toe-curlingly strong espresso and cappuccino made with four different kinds of coffee beans and topped with steamed milk and cocoa. Nor does it need any introduction to the North End teenagers and waterfront condo dwellers who flock here for such traditional Italian sweets as *torta di ricotta* (cheese pie) and lucious *cannoli* (crisp fried dough tubes filled with whipped, sweetened ricotta).

Founded by Avelino-born Oscar DeStefano and family in 1976, the Paradiso is one of the rare places in the North End where you will still find handmade spumoni and freshly churned Italian ices. The latter include both *gelati* (Italian ice cream with less butterfat than American ice cream) and *granita* (delicate Italian sherbet that melts on your tongue like a snowflake). Gelati flavors range from predictable chocolate and raspberry to exotic nutmeg, while the lemon granita is so fresh, you sometimes bite a seed!

The decor of the Caffe Paradiso might be described as "New Age bordello," consisting of track lights, hanging plants, and mirrors and mirrored tables everywhere. The crowds and blaring jukebox make conversation a challenge. The elegant dining room upstairs serves authentic Italian fare that's a cut above most in the North End.

CHANG FENG

Rating: ★★

Type of cuisine: Chinese (Mandarin/Szechuan)

Price range: appetizers $2.00–4.00; entrees $3.00–6.00

289 Beacon St., Somerville

Telephone: 864–6265

Hours: open for lunch Tuesday–Friday from 11:30 a.m.–2 p.m.; for dinner Tuesday–Sunday from 4:30 p.m.–10 p.m.

No reservations

No credit cards

BYOB

Wheelchair access fair

Dress: casual

It's hard to say who fares better at this tiny Chinese restaurant, the sit-down customers or the people who come here for take-out. The former endure waits of up to 40 minutes in a line that, nightly, curls around the front of this unassuming Somerville storefront, while the latter have to eat their delectable Szechuan and Mandarin stir-fries less than optimally piping hot. You won't find either group complaining, however, because Chang Feng's vegetables are a little crisper, its ginger is a little spicier, and its prices are a little lower than almost any other Chinese restaurant in town.

The pint-sized Chang Feng (the name translates "rising wind") was founded not by a Chinese, but by Vietnamese-born Alphonse Dao, who, together with two sisters, has run the restaurant since 1975. His birthplace notwithstanding, Dao certainly knows his Chinese cooking—spicing up cold sliced pork with tangy garlic sauce, stir-frying beef with crisp green peppers and fresh orange peel, preparing cashew nut chicken, a Szechuan favorite, with cashews the size of walnuts. Vegetarians appreciate the meatless *chow mein* and *moo shi* with vegetables, the latter served with crepe-like pancakes used for scooping up the filling. Everyone appreciates the low-priced lunch which features fried rice, barbecued chicken wings, and a daily changing stir-fry, not to mention a hot and sour soup chock full of lily buds and wood ears.

The dining room, with its Chinese lanterns and grey linoleum floor, is not what you would call elegant, but that in no way diminishes the demand for one of the 40 red cane chairs at the mismatched formica tables.

CHARLIE'S SANDWICH SHOPPE

Rating: ★★

Type of cuisine: American/breakfast

Price range: cheap

429 Columbus Ave., Boston

Telephone: 536–7669

Hours: open Monday–Friday from 6 a.m.–2:30 p.m.; Saturday 7:30 a.m.–2:30 p.m.

No reservations

No credit cards

No liquor license

Wheelchair access good

Dress: casual

Boston has changed considerably since Sammy Davis Jr., Duke Ellington, and other visiting performers came to this venerable South End luncheonette, one of the few restaurants, in those days, where blacks were welcomed. But at the legendary Charlie's, time has all but stood still. The red swivel stools still line the time-worn lunch counter, cardboard signs over the stove list the daily specials, and now, as then, freshly baked muffins and billowy biscuits still fill the tiny shop window.

Today, Charlie's draws a diverse clientele ranging from day laborers and South End old-timers to briefcase-toting young professionals. But class differences are forgotten over some of Boston's freshest eggs and hash browns, blueberry pancakes so juicy they squirt when you cut into them, and sandwiches as low in price as they are fat with fillings. Charlie's is also one of the few places around where you can dine on turkey hash! The homemade mincemeat and sweet potato pies are also worth gobbling.

CHIEKO

Rating: ★★

Type of cuisine: Japanese

Price range: appetizers from $2.50–5.00; entrees $5.00–9.00

132 College Ave., Somerville

Telephone: 623–9263

Hours: open for dinner Sunday and Tuesday–Thursday from 5–9:45 p.m.; Friday–Saturday till 10:45 p.m.

Reservations accepted, but not usually needed

No credit cards

BYOB

Wheelchair access good

Dress: casual

I have never understood why Chieko isn't more crowded. This family-run restaurant serves some of the cheapest and tastiest Japanese food in greater Boston. True, Somerville might be the last place you would expect to find a decent Japanese restaurant, but do take advantage of this out-of-the-way location to avoid the waiting lines and parking problems encountered at most of the downtown Japanese establishments.

Run by Tokyo-born Chieko Finn ("I am really Irish," she jokes in a heavy Japanese accent), Chieko specializes in Japanese home-style cooking. You could begin with an appetizer of *tempura* (light, batter-fried shrimp and vegetables) or perhaps *yakitori* (tiny kebabs threaded with onions and marinated chicken). The tiny sushi bar (and, come to think of it, this is the first place I have seen a woman sushi chef) prides itself on its *futomaki* (brightly colored, pickled Japanese vegetables rolled up with vinegared rice and seaweed), a popular item with vegetarians from nearby Tufts University.

The entrees may not strike you as a bargain until you realize that the price includes *miso* (fermented soy bean) soup, tart cabbage salad, sweet omelette appetizer, rice, tea and dessert. Main courses range from teriyaki beef or chicken (broiled with a sweet-salt sauce and served with stir-fried bean sprouts) to *tonkatsu* (an audibly crisp, deep-fried pork chop served with hot, salty cabbage). The sushi selection here is limited but Chieko is one of the few places that carries fresh "sweet red" shrimp from Maine. The adventurous can try *chirashi sushi* (a lacquerware bowl of rice topped with a colorful array of raw fish, pickled vegetables, and seaweed). (Note: In general, the sushi is better at the larger, downtown Japanese restaurants.) Dessert consists of orange sherbet or creamy ginger ice cream and is included with the price of dinner.

Chieko's 40-seat dining room is decorated with colorful Japanese kites and cascades of origami sparrows. A birdcage-like entryway divides the storefront into two intimate dining areas, one with a three-seat sushi bar.

COFFEE CONNECTION

Rating: ★★½

Type of cuisine: coffee house/desserts and light fare

Price range: cheap

36 Boylston St. (in the Garage in Harvard Square), Cambridge

Telephone: 492–4881

Hours: open Monday–Thursday from 8 a.m.–midnight; Friday till 1 a.m.; Saturday from 9 a.m.–1 a.m.; Sunday from 9 a.m.–midnight

No reservations

Major credit cards accepted

No liquor

Wheelchair access adequate

Dress: casual

Any place that sells a ton and a half of beans each week has the right idea about coffee. No wonder this animated Harvard Square coffee house has for five straight years received *Boston Magazine*'s "Best of Boston" award for its potent espresso, frothy cappuccino (espresso topped with steamed milk, cinnamon, and grated chocolate), and C.O.D. ("coffee of the day") served in individual Melior pots (simply plunge the filter to the bottom of the glass cylinder when the coffee is brewed to the strength you desire).

The Coffee Connection was founded in 1975 by a caffeine addict named George Howell, who understood that the secret to a good cup of coffee lay as much in freshly roasting the beans as in grinding and brewing them to order. To achieve the ultimate cup, he purchased a coffee roaster from Germany and personally began roasting each of the 18 to 20 varieties of beans sold at the Coffee Connection. Howell's coffee selections range from Brazilian *santos* ("mellow acidity . . . with a sweet 'mocha' flavor," says the menu) to Yemeni *mocha mattari* ("wonderfully complex—bittersweet flavor") to New Orleans roast ("strong dark roast flavor without too much bitterness"). Tea lovers will find more than 30 different brews to choose from. The light menu features homemade granola for breakfast, cheese boards and a "dill thrill" (vegetables and Havarti cheese on French bread with cucumber dill dressing) for lunch. Superlative desserts served around the clock include chocolaty Sacher torte, cheesecake with walnut crust, and the densest, richest, moistest gingerbread that I have tasted anywhere.

Located in the glass-and-brick-lined Galleria in Harvard Square, the Coffee Connection boasts a contemporary decor of arched windows, exposed brick, and overhead trellises. Cherry-wood tables are crowded into a two-tiered dining area; the walls are decorated with colorful yarn paintings by the Latin American artist Jose Benitez Sanchez. Unlike other Cambridge coffee houses, the Coffee Connection would have to be characterized as bustling rather than mellow. An adjacent retail shop will supply your carry-out needs.

DAILY CATCH

Rating: ★★½

Type of cuisine: Italian/seafood

Price range: appetizers $2.00–4.00; entrees $7.00–10.00

323 Hanover St., Boston

Telephone: 523–8567

Hours: open Wednesday–Saturday from 11:30 a.m.–10:30 p.m.;
Sunday–Tuesday from 5–10 p.m.

No reservations (expect a wait)

No credit cards

BYOB

Wheelchair access good

Dress: informal

A recent visit to the tiny Daily Catch found chef Wendy Daniels peeling garlic into a mostly full, six-quart container. "Your supply for the year?" we asked nervously. "For the week!" replied the youthful chef of this popular North End seafood house. Yes, the profligate use of garlic is one reason why the Daily Catch is not for the faint-hearted, and so is the house specialty, squid.

Squid or *calamari*, as it is called in Italian, has a delicate shellfish flavor and the resiliency of very *al dente* pasta. At the Daily Catch this tentacled sea creature is served fried, sautéed, stuffed (with Italian cold cuts and pine nuts), as a salad, in red sauce or white sauce with linguini, and even in the form of "meatballs." Fortunately for finicky eaters, calamari is only part of the story because the chowder made with freshly shucked clams, the broiled scrod, and copious house salad are excellent, too. Why, they even have a dish of haute culinary pretension in the form of lobster *fra diavolo*. For dessert you have to go elsewhere: may I suggest the nearby Caffe Paradiso (see p. 87).

The bread-box-sized dining room has the Old World charm of checkered tablecloths, sawdust-strewn floor, and seating for 20. You can't help but watch your food being prepared because the stove stands in the center of the dining area; indeed, much of the food is served in the skillet in which it was cooked. The restroom, by the way, is located in the café across the street.

DURGIN-PARK

Rating: ★★½

Type of cuisine: New England/American

Price range: appetizers $0.75–5.00; entrees $5.00–12.00

340 South Building, Faneuil Hall Market Place, Boston

Telephone: 227–2038

Hours: open Monday–Saturday from 11:30 a.m.–10 p.m.; Sunday from noon–9 p.m.

No reservations

No credit cards

Full bar

Wheelchair access poor

Dress: casual

Don't even dream about leisurely dining at this restaurant. Everything about the legendary Durgin-Park is designed to make you rush through dinner. A mandatory 30–45 minute wait for a table sharpens your hunger and, when you order, your food is delivered almost before you've closed the menu. The cacophony of the other guests and of the waitresses thundering down the narrow aisles like basketball players makes lengthy conversation impossible. Naturally, you'll bolt your food, but don't worry, you're supposed to. The name of the game at Durgin-Park is volume and on a typical Saturday night, between the hours of 5 and 9 p.m., the restaurant will serve a mind-boggling 1000 guests.

This venerable restaurant was founded by John Durgin, Eldridge Park, and a third partner, John Chandler, in 1827, when Quincy Market was an honest-to-God produce market. Now, as then, its chief attraction is the vast portions of solid Yankee fare at astonishingly low prices. At this writing, oysters cost less than four bits each and $1 will fetch a bowl of buttery fish chowder. In an age when boutique restaurants charge $18 for a few snippets of duck breast, Durgin-Park sells a whole half duck, loaded with bread stuffing and slathered with gravy, for a paltry $7.

The real showstopper at Durgin-Park is the prime rib, a blood-rare, bible-thick slab with a bone the size of a barrel stave. Avoid the gristly swordfish tips but don't miss the buttery scallops. Side dishes range from delectable squash and onion rings to baked beans that ought to be better for a restaurant with this much history. Excellent cornbread is supposed to accompany the entrees so don't be afraid to ask for it if your waitress forgets. But whatever you order, save room for the Indian pudding and homemade strawberry shortcake, both so tasty, you'll forgive the indelicacies of the service.

Durgin-Park may be the only Quincy Market area restaurant that does *not* have hanging ferns, exposed brick, or expanses of butcher block. The dining rooms, with their worn plank floors, embossed tin ceilings, and sickly yellow walls, have remained unchanged from the way they looked decades ago. The tables, draped with red checkered tablecloths, seat 16, so don't come here for that intimate *tête à tête*. The long waiting line can be abridged, if not entirely avoided, by having a few drinks in the bar. Tell the bartender you would like to have dinner and he'll send you directly to the dining room via a hidden staircase when a table opens up. There is also a raw bar in the basement where ill-tempered shuckers serve tasty oysters and steamers. The house beer is dark and delicious. Not all the waitresses live up to their battle-axe reputations; on a recent visit ours was as demure as could be.

LA ESPAGNOLA

Rating: ★★

Type of cuisine: Cuban

Price range: cheap

405 Center St., Jamaica Plain

Telephone: 524–9410

Hours: open seven days a week from noon–10:30 p.m.

No reservations

No credit cards

BYOB

Wheelchair access good

Dress: casual

Center St. in Jamaica Plain may not be the most auspicious location for a restaurant but don't let the tawdry environs of La Espagnola put you off too much. This tiny storefront remains one of the great wonders of the culinary world: how *do* they manage to serve such great Cuban food at prices inversely proportional to the huge size of the portions?

La Espagnola makes and bottles its own hot sauce, a fiery elixir that tastes every bit as good in the dinner rolls as it does on the *ensalada verde* ("green salad" garnished with string beans, avocado, and cucumber). The *sopa* (full-flavored broth loaded with beef and vegetables) could well make a meal in itself, but do eat it sparingly to save room for the *pollo guizado* (chicken stewed to fall-off-the-bone tenderness). Fish lovers will wish to try the *pescado guizado* (kingfish steaks topped with onions, peppers, and tomato sauce) or perhaps the *calamares en su tinta* (cuttle-fish simmered with herbs in its own ink). Vegetables include *fried plantain* (a soft sweet fruit that tastes like a cross between a banana and a potato) and *moro* (black beans and rice) which taste better together than either would taste separately. Desserts are designed for the sweet tooth and range from moist *flan* (caramel custard) to cheesecake with gooey pineapple topping. Sucrophiles will likewise relish the Latin American soft drinks which come in such flavors as coconut and *tamarind* (a tart brown fruit).

La Espagnola's postage-stamp-sized-dining room boasts rec room paneling, plastic skylights, and 10 tidy tables covered with flowered oilcloth. Access to the restroom is gained through the family-run kitchen. Brown-bagging is the norm: there is a package store across the street to the left.

GALERIA UMBERTO

Rating: ★★

Type of cuisine: pizza, calzone, and other Italian fingerfood

Price range: under $1 per item

289 Hanover St., Boston

No telephone

Hours: open for lunch Monday–Saturday from 11 a.m.–2:30 p.m.; closed during July

No reservations—long waiting lines

No credit cards

Beer and wine

Wheelchair access good

Dress: casual

Who ever heard of a pizzeria that only opens at lunchtime? This cavernous, North End lunch spot is so popular that it can afford to stay closed between the hours of 2:30 p.m.–11 a.m. and during the entire month of July—the height of Boston's tourist season! The first impression to greet you on entering the Galeria Umberto is the perfume of freshly baked bread dough. If you're lucky, you will only have to spend 20 minutes in line with Italian school kids before you assuage your hunger.

The pizza, parcelled out by knife-wielding muscle men, is not the pepperoni-and-anchovy sort served at university neighborhood pizzerias but Neapolitan-style, a moist slab of bread dough smeared with tomato sauce and cheese. But do save room for such less familiar delicacies as *calzone* (spinach and cheese-filled turnovers), *panini* (spiral-shaped rolls filled with cold cuts), and *panzorotti* (potato dumplings with delectable deep-fried crusts). *Arincini* means "little oranges," literally, but these orange-shaped balls are made from cheese-filled, deep-fried rice. The *pizzetta* may look like sticky buns but the "sugar" glaze on top of these meat-stuffed rolls is actually melted cheese. This spicy fare can produce a powerful thirst, so it's fortunate that beer and wine are served in disposable plastic cups. The best news of all is the prices: why, Gargantua himself could fill up for less than $5!

The Galeria Umberto's decor is not its best feature but the travel posters and huge painting of the boot of Italy do lend a feel for the Old Country. The bakery branch of the Galeria Umberto sells fresh Italian bread and pizza from a steamy basement on Parmenter St.

HARVARD DO-NUT SHOP

Rating: ★½

Type of cuisine: American breakfast and lunch (muffins the house specialty)

Price range: cheap

647 Mass. Ave., Cambridge

Telephone: 491-8231

Hours: open Monday–Saturday from 5:30 a.m.–7 p.m., closed Sunday

No reservations

No credit cards

No liquor

Wheelchair access fine

Dress: casual

The name of this bustling luncheonette is misleading because the house specialty is not doughnuts but muffins—great billowy cakes served in staggering profusion. At last count, the Harvard Do-Nut Shop sold some 35 different kinds of muffins, ranging from predictable bran, cranberry, and blueberry (the best seller) to exotic carrot, pistachio, and even peanut butter-chocolate chip. For the last 21 years, Harvard Do-Nut owner Bob LeBlanc has reigned as Central Square's muffin king and his repertory changes constantly to suit the tastes, however bizarre (my favorite is squash-raisin), of his customers.

At the client's request, muffins are split, toasted on the grill, and served on a plastic plate with margarine. Should muffins not be to your liking, you'll find here such typical greasy spoon fare as bacon and egg platters, grilled cheese sandwiches, and hot dogs. The soup, I am sorry to say, is Campbell's.

Harvard Do-Nut draws a motley assortment of Central Square office workers, hard hats, and bag ladies. Thousands of elbows have worn spots in the long formica counter and countless cups of coffee "regulah" have been sipped at the brown leather stools and 6 wooden booths that line the narrow serving area. The customers, most of them regulars, address the waitresses, most of them veterans, by first name, and a jukebox in the back provides music.

HERRELL'S

Rating: ★★

Type of cuisine: ice cream

Price range: cheap

15 Dunster St., Cambridge

Telephone: 497–2179

Hours: open Sunday–Thursday from noon–midnight; Friday and Saturday till 1 a.m.

No reservations

No credit cards

No liquor

Wheelchair access fair

Dress: casual

I have never understood why ice cream manufacturers strive to create new flavors. To me, the subject of frozen desserts begins and ends with chocolate. I used to think that the best chocolate ice cream in Boston was the one I made with six egg yolks to a quart of milk in my Proctor and Silex ice cream machine. That was before I tasted the chocolate pudding ice cream at the newly opened Herrell's in Harvard Square.

The Herrell of this side street ice cream parlor is Steve Herrell, founder of the legendary Steve's in Somerville. After four years of spectacular success, not to mention increasingly acrimonious labor disputes, Steve sold his name and popular ice cream parlor to Joey Crugnale (see p. 105), who promptly opened a chain of Steve's around Boston. (To judge from the long waiting lines, the masses do not share my opinion that the quality of Steve's ice cream has plummeted.) Meanwhile, the original Steve returned to the ice cream business, opening a Herrell's in Northampton, Massachusetts in 1980. By December, 1982, there was a Herrell's in Harvard Square with plans to open a third store in Somerville's Union Square in the coming months.

Herrell built his reputation on "mix-ins" which are now called "smoosh-ins"; ice cream kneaded with pieces of Heath Bar, M & M's, Oreo cookies, and other snacks. Other ice cream flavors here include mocha, malted vanilla, almond cream, and peanut butter chocolate (I guess some people will eat anything with chocolate in it). Housed in a former bank building, Herrell's eating area boasts marble tabletops and a garish submarine wall painting. There's a smaller dining area in what was formerly the bank vault.

HILLTOP STEAK HOUSE

Rating: ★½

Type of cuisine: meat and potatoes

Price range: entrees $5.00–10.00

855 Broadway (Route 1), Saugus

Telephone: 233–7700

Hours: open seven days a week from 11 a.m.–11 p.m.

No reservations

No credit cards

Full bar

Wheelchair access adequate

Dress: casual

The Hilltop restaurant needs no introduction, at least not to the hungry hordes who daily turn in at the huge neon cactus, park in the vast 1000-vehicle parking lot, and take their places in the waiting line, not unlike the plastic cows that graze in front of this steak house. I wouldn't call the Hilltop a restaurant (a factory or feeding station, perhaps), nor would I again endure the 40-minute wait for a table in a bar with a merciless air conditioner and public address system that noisily orders guests to the various dining rooms. But like Boston's Anthony's Pier 4 or the No Name, this behemoth eatery must be experienced once in a lifetime. And for many of the 1400 customers that can simultaneously be seated here, the Hilltop is a weekly ritual.

Any restaurant that goes through twenty tractor-trailer loads of beef loins a week has the right idea about meat and, although you might find more tender or well-aged beef elsewhere, you certainly won't get more for your money. The tenderloin is as big as a softball and the sirloin steak as thick as the Boston yellow pages. Other house specialties include stuffed and baked lobster pie, breaded cutlets, broiled pork chops, and chopped sirloin, the last three available in half portions for children. Appetizers have been streamlined to juices and fruit cups in an effort to shorten the time the customer spends at the table. Desserts bring out the child in all of us, ranging from jello to homemade apple pie to delicious grapenut pudding topped with whipped cream. The dressing on the salad (mostly iceberg lettuce) is sufficiently popular to warrant its sale in bottles.

The dining rooms, seating 100 to 400 people, bear such Wild West names as Kansas City, Dodge City, and Sioux City—the latter boasts a 28-foot fieldstone fireplace. The decor consists of Tiffany-style lamps, cowboy prints, and wooden Indians—all as new as a shiny penny.

HOODOO BARBECUE

Rating: ★★½

Type of cuisine: barbecue

Price range: cheap

528 Commonwealth Ave., Boston

Telephone: 247–8267

Hours: open Sunday–Thursday from 11 a.m.–9 p.m.; Friday and
Saturday till 10 p.m.

No reservations

No credit cards

Full bar

Wheelchair access good

Entertainment: live punk rock nightly in the discotheque downstairs

Dress: casual

There exists among connoisseurs of spareribs a strange inverse snobbery
concerning the restaurants that serve them. Thus, a rib joint that serves
on paper plates is usually more highly regarded than one that serves on
china, while service on waxed paper is the most highly regarded of all.
You can't get more low life than the Hoodoo Barbecue located above a
punk rock nightclub popularly known as the "Rat," but neither will you
find better ribs in Boston.

Hoodoo owner James Ryan doesn't mess around with dainty
Canadian baby back ribs, serving pork ribs, lamb ribs (my favorite), and
beef ribs the size of barrel staves, each crisply charred under the broiler.
What distinguishes the ribs at the Hoodoo is the tongue-searing barbecue
sauce made with ketchup, molasses, liquid smoke, and believe it or not,
vanilla. The ribs come with a slice of balloon bread for mopping up the
sauce. Should you still be hungry afterward (unlikely), the Hoodoo serves
very respectable barbecued chicken, potato salad, and sweet potato pie for
dessert.

The Hoodoo occupies the ground floor of a bar called the
Rathskeller, a punk rock gathering spot by night and a BU watering hole
by day. An antique wood bar runs the length of the restaurant which is

further accoutered with video games and a jukebox that snarls such melodies as "I Want to Be Sedated" by the Ramones. Don't be too put off by the surroundings: after all, the Hoodoo Barbecue was named one of the hundred best new restaurants in the United States by *Esquire Magazine* in 1981!

HO YUEN TING

Rating: ★★½

Type of cuisine: Chinese (Cantonese)

Price range: entrees $4.00–7.00

13A Hudson St., Boston

Telephone: 426–2316

Hours: open Thursday–Saturday, Monday and Tuesday from noon–9:30 p.m.; Sunday from 3:30–9:30 p.m.; closed Wednesday

No reservations

No credit cards

BYOB

Wheelchair access poor

Dress: casual

The management recently raised the prices at this casual Chinatown eatery; it now costs $30 for a party of four to gorge themselves to oblivion! Then again, $7.50 per person for a meal of watercress soup, beef *chow foon*, and a spectacular whole steamed bass with tangy black bean sauce is not what I would call excessively expensive. The low prices are only part of what draws capacity crowds to this steamy basement; the high percentage of Chinese customers here attests to the authenticity of Ho Yuen Ting's Cantonese bill of fare.

Soups are served in family-style tureens (the "small" size will comfortably feed three) ranging from familiar, tangy watercress soup to exotic salted-vegetable-bean-curd soup made with peppery preserved Chinese vegetables. Other house specialties include chicken *kew*, "eight treasure" *chow foon* (chewy rice noodles garnished with roast pork, chicken giblets, shrimp, squid, abalone, and Chinese vegetables), and a whole steamed fish flavored with ginger, scallions, and soy sauce. There's no wine list but brown bagging is cheerfully tolerated. (You can pick up your favorite Chinese alcoholic beverages at the nearby Essex Liquor Store at 15–17 Essex St.)

Ho Yuen Ting makes most Chinatown restaurants seem opulent, consisting of a single, bare-bones dining room with a mere forty seats. A potted palm and a radiator serve as the room's only ornaments—and they are usually obscured by the crowds of people waiting for a table.

IMPERIAL TEAHOUSE

Rating: ★★

Type of cuisine: dim sum/Cantonese

Price range: cheap for *dim sum*; à la carte entrees $4.50–15.00

70 Beech St., Boston

Telephone: 426–8439

Hours: open seven days a week from 9 a.m.–1 a.m.

No reservations for *dim sum*

Major credit cards accepted

Full bar

Wheelchair access poor

Entertainment: no entertainment as such, but the serving of *dim sum* can be pretty dramatic

Dress: casual

"*Dim sum*, lose some," might be an apt saying for Chinatown. *Dim sum* means "bits and pieces eaten at odd moments to please the heart" literally, referring to a traditional Chinese mid-morning meal comprised of dozens of different kinds of dumplings, noodle dishes, soups, and steamed and fried pastries. *Dim sum* proves a novel way to assuage your hunger while sparing your pocketbook and no place offers a wider variety than the Imperial Teahouse in the heart of Chinatown.

Dim sum is served in the second floor dining room of the Imperial Teahouse, a vast hall with the coffered ceilings, sculpted dragons, and Chinese lanterns of a Forbidden City palace. Take a seat by a window overlooking Beech St., Chinatown's main artery, and enjoy the show. Soon a cart loaded with delicacies will halt at your table and, as there are no menus, you order by pointing with your chopsticks to whatever looks good. *Dim sum* range from familiar spareribs and spring rolls (the latter smaller and crisper than most in Chinatown) to exotic *chung-tzu* (garnished steamed rice wrapped in lotus leaf). Newcomers may wish to start with *har gao* (opalescent shrimp dumplings), *shao mai* (pork-shrimp meatballs), or *pork bao* (steamed buns filled with barbecued pork). The adventurous can test their mettle with such exotica as curried squid, tripe with black bean sauce, and chicken feet braised in soy sauce. To figure the tab, the waiter simply tallies the number of empty serving plates on the table. Don't worry about ordering something you don't like; the prices are low enough so that you don't have to clean your plate.

Dim sum at the Imperial Teahouse is served daily between the hours of 9 a.m. and 3 p.m. It is best to arrive early to avoid the invariably long waiting lines. A full menu of Cantonese dishes is served in the dining room downstairs.

JOEY'S

Rating: ★★½

Type of cuisine: ice cream

Price range: cheap

1161 Broadway St., Somerville

Telephone: 623–9013

Hours: open daily from 1 p.m.–midnight

No reservations

No credit cards

No liquor

Wheelchair access good

Dress: casual

Somerville may not be renowned for its restaurants but this northwest township, home to a sizable student population, has been the starting point of many a local ice cream empire. It was here, in Davis Square, that Steve Herrell (see p. 99) opened a storefront parlor equipped with a rumbling churn in the window that was destined to become the legendary Steve's. It was also here, near Teal Square, that Joey Crugnale opened Joey's, the ice cream shop chosen by *Boston Magazine* to represent Boston in the first National Ice Cream Taste-Off, sponsored by *Philadelphia Magazine* on July 8, 1982. Joey's vanilla finished a cool ninth in the contest but the chocolate cinnamon raisin made a very respectable showing among the nation's top flavored ice creams. The chocolate cinnamon raisin ice cream leads me to consider Joey's Boston's best ice cream parlor and at no point is my freezer without a quart of it.

As befits an ice cream shop, chocolate figures prominently in the house specialties which include chocolate almond, Oreo cookie, and even chocolate banana. The espresso will delight coffee lovers and the malted vanilla is equally delicious, its flavor reminiscent of an English treat, Horlick's tablets. Unique to Joey's is a sundae bar that allows you to dress up a dish of ice cream with fresh bananas, crumbled Reese's peanut butter cups, and all-you-can-eat aerosol whipped cream.

Joey's is probably the most atmospheric of Boston's ice cream parlors. Its high ceilings are faced with embossed tin and Tiffany-style lamps and its walls are decorated with antique drugstore signs. If you're lucky, you can sit at one of the oak tables; if you're not, you take a seat on a stool at the back of the shop. The youthful staff gyrates to the beat of loud disco music; indulge them as they make it a point of pride to pack the take-out containers as full of ice cream as possible.

KEBAB-N-KURRY

Rating: ★★½

Type of cuisine: Indian

Price range: appetizers $1.50–2.00; entrees $4.50–8.00

30 Massachusetts Avenue, Boston

Telephone: 536-9835

Hours: open Monday–Friday noon–2 p.m. and 5–10 p.m.; Saturday noon–3 p.m. and 5–10 p.m.

Reservations accepted

Major credit cards accepted

BYOB

Wheelchair access poor

Dress: casual

O.K., so it *does* sound like a fast food joint in New Delhi. Don't be misled by the cutesy name, because this homey hole-in-the-wall serves the best Northern Indian food in Boston.

Kebab-N-Kurry was opened in 1980 by Vinod and Shakila Kapoor, both natives of New Delhi. "Not all Indian food is hot," insist the young couple and to prove it they serve six different kinds of curry ranging from mild *saag* (delicately spiced curry with spinach) and *korma* (a mildly spiced almond and cream curry) to the admittedly incendiary *vindaloo*. The kebabs are no ordinary shish kebabs but authentic *tandoori* (meat or seafood marinated in spice paste to a mercurochrome orange, then grilled over glowing charcoals).

Begin your meal here with *pakoras* (deep-fried, chickpea batter-coated vegetables) or *samosas* (potato turnovers) served with mint chutney. For desserts, try *gulab jamun* (doughnut holes doused with syrup) or *ras malai* (sweet, fresh cheese balls perfumed with pistachio nuts and rose water).

Along the way, be sure to sample some traditional Indian breads, like puffed, deep-fried *poori* or *papadom* (a potato-chip-like bread made from lentils). *Raita* (cool yogurt cucumber dip) will help you to extinguish the fires.

Kebab-N-Kurry occupies a cozy basement painted peach and furnished with tables for 40. They don't have a liquor license, so don't forget to load up on beer at the liquor store across the street. Believe me, you'll need it!

KOREA HOUSE RESTAURANT

Rating: ★★½

Type of cuisine: Korean

Price range: appetizers $2.50–8.50; entrees $5.50–10.00

20 Pearl St., Cambridge

Telephone: 492–9643

Hours: open Monday–Saturday from noon to 10 p.m.

Reservations recommended for the Korean dining room

No credit cards

BYOB

Wheelchair access good

Dress: casual

Sandwiched between Japan and China, Korea lies at the culinary cross-roads of the Orient. The food at Cambridge's Korea House Restaurant recalls the fiery spicing of Szechuan food and the Japanese flair for preparing seafood and noodle dishes, but the style of cooking remains uniquely Korean.

This bright Central Square storefront specializes in family-style Korean cooking, the filling soups and stir-fries that its largely Asian clientele (many MIT students) grew up on. *Mandoo-kui* (pan-fried, meat- and vegetable-filled dumplings) are the house specialty and are served with piquant dipping sauce as an appetizer or in a hardy broth with vegetables as a main course soup. Other typical Korean dishes here include *bool-go-ki* (marinated, barbecued sliced beef) *gal-bee gui* (barbecued short ribs), *sang sun-chi gai* (Korean bouillabaisse), and *naemg myun* (an intriguing dish of cold noodles with beef broth and cucumbers, served in a shining silver bowl).

Delicious as the Korea House entrees are, don't overlook such side dishes as seasoned and spiced bean sprouts, seasoned and spiced spinach (both laced with sesame seeds and served cold), and *kim chi* (Korean sauerkraut—pickled Chinese cabbage ignited with chili). Nutty "twig" tea is served with dinner and wine or beer can be purchased at nearby Libby's Liquors, 575 Mass. Ave. Koreans do not customarily eat sweets after dinner so dessert requires another trip around the corner, this time to the Vouros Pastry Shop, 480 Mass. Ave., where baklava and other Greek pastries can be enjoyed with muddy Greek coffee.

Run by Seoul-born Chung Soo Chin, Korea House moved to its present location in July, 1972, from the storefront it formerly occupied in Newton Center. The left half of the small dining room is furnished with chairs and white formica-topped tables; the right side, separated by bamboo screens, has a raised dais and low tables for eating Korean-style (sitting cross-legged). Remember to remove your shoes before entering. Both dining rooms are decorated with a cheerful combination of lamp-light, fresh flower sprays, scroll paintings, and other Oriental handicrafts.

LALIBELA

Rating: ★½

Type of cuisine: Ethiopian

Price range: entrees $5.00–7.00

333 Massachusetts Ave., Boston

Telephone: 247–9276

Hours: open Tuesday–Sunday from 11 a.m.–10 p.m.

Reservations usually not necessary

No credit cards

BYOB

Wheelchair access adequate

Dress: casual

This Ethiopian restaurant, to date the only one of its kind in Boston, is for people who haven't outgrown the pleasure of eating with their fingers. All the food here is served on huge, millet flour pancakes called *injera* and the name of the game is to tear off a small piece and use it to scoop up your food (not unlike eating Chinese *moo shi*). Don't fret too much about mastering the technique beforehand because the waitresses are only too happy to show you how to eat like a native.

Unusual as it is, Ethiopian cooking does share common points with the cuisines of North Africa and Asia. The popularity of lamb and wheat pilaf suggests an Arabic influence while the intense spicing recalls the fiery curries of India. The precise blending of flavors and the eating style are unique.

On your first visit to Lalibela you might start with *yebeg alitcha* (mild lamb stew with potatoes) then work your way up to *yebeg khe wott* (spicy lamb stew) or *tibs* (fried beef with onions, rosemary, and fiery whipped pepper paste). Happily, sour cream is provided for dipping to help extinguish the fires. Vegetarians can order *mesir wott*, lentil stew, or *kinche* (buttery wheat pilaf) while die-hard carnivores can try the *kitfo* (warm, tough raw beef—a taste that I have yet to acquire).

Named for a famous Ethiopian ruler, this bare-bones eatery faces Symphony Hall. The decor consists of Ethiopian travel posters, less-than-immaculate tables separated by office partitions, and wicker baskets suspended from the ceiling like a skyful of flying saucers. Recorded Ethiopian music lends a measure of local color. The service is amicable and leisurely.

LAST CHANCE CAFE

Rating: ★½

Type of cuisine: health food

Price range: entrees under $5.00

25 Central Square, Cambridge

Telephone: 547–8551

Hours: open Monday–Friday from 11 a.m.–8 p.m.; Saturday till 8 p.m.

No reservations

No credit cards

BYOB

Wheelchair access tight

Dress: casual

The Last Chance Café may be the smallest restaurant in Boston, but the coffee house intimacy created by its red velvet curtains, barnboard walls, and 16 handmade tables is only part of what makes it one of my favorite places to eat health food. The Last Chance is an oasis amid the pizza joints, blaring radios, and rumbling trucks of Central Square—a quiet place where, during off hours at least, you can linger over coffee and a newspaper (preferably the *Cambridge Chronicle* or *Equal Times*).

The Last Chance has a daily changing menu (see the blackboard) of macrobiotic and vegetarian specialties. Health-minded fast food fans may wish to try some tofu sausage (made with smoked bean curd—it's delicious) or perhaps a "solar burger" (a ground wheat and soybean patty served on whole wheat bread with lettuce, tomato, and mayo). Salads feature romaine lettuce (not iceberg), festooned with alfalfa sprouts and creamy sesame-tofu dressing. Last Chance desserts range from squash pie with visible specks of spices to warm pear crunch topped with nut-loaded, homemade granola. To assuage your thirst, there is sugarless soda pop, not to mention *bancha* (twig tea) and coffee. Mercifully, sugar is available on request for heretics like me.

Located in a former White Tower Hamburger building, the Last Chance is operated by Hiroshi Hayashi, who also owns Latacarta and the Seventh Inn. It's a good thing they do a carry-out business because the miniscule dining room would never meet the demands of its Cantabridgian clients. To place your order, step up to the open kitchen in the middle of the dining room. And don't forget to sprinkle your pan-fried rice or noodles with the soy sauce, sesame seeds, and Japanese chili powder provided in place of mustard and ketchup.

MANDALAY

Rating: ★★★

Type of cuisine: Burmese/Chinese

Price range: appetizers $2.50–4.00; entrees $4.00–8.00

329 Huntington Ave., Boston

Telephone: 247–2111

Hours: open Monday–Friday from 11:30 a.m.–10:30 p.m. (special lunch menu from 11:30 a.m.–2:30 p.m.); Saturday and Sunday from 5–11:30 p.m.

Reservations accepted

Credit cards accepted

Beer and wine

Wheelchair access poor

Dress: casual

At the risk of sounding older than I really am, I remember the Mandalay before it was a proper restaurant. The Rangoon-born Chin family had just opened what was to be the Bay State's first Burmese restaurant in a former soda shop in a rundown Huntington Avenue basement. The tables were jammed around the ice cream counter, decor was non-existent, and to reach the restroom you had to walk through the kitchen. All of these drawbacks seemed to be minor inconveniences considering the low prices and spicy succulence of the food.

Over the years the Mandalay has become a proper restaurant complete with prettily set tables, walls decorated with textured paper and Burmese folk art, and an attractive display of Burmese handicrafts in a showcase by the door. The new wine list makes brown bagging unnecessary and the Mandalay's proximity to Symphony Hall remains an enticement for music lovers seeking an unusual but reliable place to dine before a concert.

Burma is located at a culinary crossroads between India, China, and Southeast Asia. An Indian influence is apparent in the Burmese fondness for curry powder and a tart fruit paste called tamarind, while the use of soy sauce, bean curd, and stir-frying recalls the venerable cooking of China. Like the Thais, the Burmese cook with salty fish sauce, pungent coriander leaf, and incendiary chilis, but in the final tally, the Mandalay's Burmese cuisine is unique. Start your meal with *sar tay* (marinated, broiled beef kebabs) or perhaps some *sar moo sar* (Burmese *kreplach*—fried dough triangles filled with curried onions and beef). The Burmese hot and sour soup has only the name (and spiciness) in common with the Szechuan version and boasts the nutty flavor of fermented bamboo shoots. The noodle dishes are excellent, too, ranging from *khawasway* (soft egg noodles with coconut cream sauce) to *lat thoke soong* (noodles tossed with vegetables and piquant tamarind). Also recommended are the *thokes* (cold salads), *chit dee kebah* (curry-filled pancakes) and, of course, the fiery house curries.

The Mandalay serves a special dinner for people who have to make an early curtain call.

MARY CHUNG

Rating: ★★½

Type of cuisine: Chinese (Szechuan/Mandarin)

Price range: appetizers from $1.00–5.00; entrees $5.00–8.00

447 Mass. Ave., Cambridge

Telephone: 864–1991

Hours: open Sunday–Thursday 11:30 a.m.–9:45 p.m.; Friday and Saturday until 10:45 p.m. *Dim Sum* (Chinese brunch) Saturday and Sunday from 11:30 a.m.–2:30 p.m.

No reservations; carry-out available

Major credit cards accepted

BYOB

Wheelchair access good

Dress: casual

It was hardly an auspicious day when a Taiwanese restaurateur named Mary Chung hung out a simple red and white sign over a narrow storefront on Mass. Ave. in Cambridge. The site, after all, had been occupied by one unremarkable Chinese restaurant after another. But as soon as people began to drift into Mary Chung to try the *suan la chow show* (plump, pork-and-herb-filled dumplings served atop crisp bean sprouts doused with chili hellfire), this humble eatery became, overnight, the number one restaurant in Boston's newest "Chinatown," Central Square.

Like most of the city's Chinese restaurants opened after 1970, Mary Chung specializes in Szechuan and Mandarin cuisine: the former, the fiery cooking of a cool, moist province in central China; the latter, a pan-national cuisine favored by a wealthy class of government officials known as mandarins. Many of Mary Chung's specialties will sear your tongue, like the *dun dun* noodles with shredded chicken (egg noodles topped with a fiery sesame paste sauce) or the "refreshing" bean sprouts (a cold appetizer stir-fried with soy sauce and tongue-blistering chili oil).

Not all the food is so incendiary, however. The delectable dry-cooked green beans with pork and crisp ham-lemon-chicken (batter-fried chicken breasts stuffed with water chestnuts and Smithfield ham, served on a bed of lettuce) can be enjoyed without danger to your digestive tract.

Other Mary Chung specialties include *ma paw tou fu* (creamy soybean curd with spicy pork sauce), *yu shiang* scallops (with a sweet-spicy sauce from the Szechuan province), and *moo shi* (crisp, stir-fried cabbage, Chinese mushrooms and a choice of shrimp, pork or chicken served with crepe-like pancakes which are wrapped around the filling). Be sure to request a dish of sweet, tangy *hoisin* sauce for spreading on the pancakes.

Mary Chung is not a stylish restaurant, consisting of a single, noisy, boxcar dining room faced with pink walls and green wainscoting. Chinese astrology charts serve as placemats and the formica-topped tables seat 40. Wine (or more appropriately, beer) can be purchased at Libby's Liquors up the street. The low prices have made Mary Chung a popular local hangout so expect a considerable wait at peak hours.

MOON VILLA

Rating: ★★

Type of cuisine: Chinese (Cantonese)

Price range: appetizers from $3.00–5.00; entrees $4.50–12.00

23 Edinboro St., Boston

Telephone: 423–2061

Hours: open daily from 9 a.m.–4 a.m.

Reservations accepted, but usually not necessary

No credit cards

BYOB

Wheelchair access poor

Dress: casual

Moon Villa has long served some of the best Cantonese food in Chinatown. But, oh, those waiters! They made Frankenstein look friendly! A few years ago I wrote something to this effect in *Boston Magazine* and, lo and behold, on subsequent visits, the staff had bcome as solicitous as a matron's butler! As for the food, any menu that lists 155 different items is bound to have a few bloopers but I still favor Moon Villa over most of the other restaurants in Chinatown.

In an age when so many Chinese chefs have jumped on the Szechuan bandwagon, it is a pleasure to find a restaurateur who stands by classical Cantonese cooking with its frank flavors untrammeled by chili hellfire. Consider Moon Villa's eight-flavor winter melon soup, a delicate broth loaded with crab, carrot, Chinese mushrooms, and winter melon (which tastes like a cross between a potato and a warm cucumber). The net result is as delicate and colorful as a watercolor. The *chow foon* (finger-thick rice noodles) have a similar succulence and are garnished with your choice of beef, barbecued pork, spareribs, or shrimp.

My favorite dishes at Moon Villa include steamed clams (cherrystones and lots of 'em) with black bean sauce, "baked ham in special chicken" (breast meat steamed with Smithfield ham and Chinese broccoli), and salt baked chicken (chicken marinated in wine, then baked in a bed of salt which leaves the bird moist but not in the slightest salty). The "individual steamed rice in pot" dishes require 45 minutes preparation time (the rice takes on a nutty flavor when baked with such intriguing garnishes as sweet Chinese sausage or squab) and is well worth the wait. (For faster service call in your order early.) Moon Villa makes few concessions to Western taste and, as a result, dishes like Chinese mushroom and fish maw soup and steamed pork with salted egg (greasy steamed pork sausage) are more apt to appeal to members of the Chinese community than to Westerners.

Moon Villa's box-like dining room is decorated with lurid orange booths and wallpaper, mirrored pillars, and seashell collages. The brown formica tables can accommodate 50. From 9 a.m. to 3 p.m., the red-coated waiters serve *dim sum* (Chinese tea pastries), among which the roast pork bun and curried beef turnover are not to be missed. Open nightly until 4 a.m., this venerable restaurant draws a loyal following of local night owls.

NADIA'S EASTERN STAR

Rating: ★★

Type of cuisine: Middle East

Price range: appetizers $2.00–5.00; entrees $6.00–9.00

280 Shawmut Avenue, Boston

Telephone: 338–8091

Hours: open seven days a week from 5 p.m. – 1 a.m.

No reservations

No credit cards

BYOB

Wheelchair access good

Dress: casual

Let me introduce you to Edna, a hefty, brassy blond waitress whose tableside manner combines the finesse of a roller derby champ with the solicitude of a Jewish grandmother! She has been at Nadia's Eastern Star since day one making sure that customers mind their manners and don't order too much food (not an easy task, considering Nadia's low prices). Edna is typical of Nadia's waitresses but don't let that scare you; she is part of what makes this informal South End eatery my favorite Middle East restaurant in town.

Nadia's Eastern Star serves what amounts to Lebanese soul food; robust dips like *hoomis* (tangy chickpea dip flavored with lemon juice and nutty *tahini*) and *baba ganooj* (made from eggplants roasted over a genuine charcoal fire). These dips are served with raw onion and plenty of fresh pita bread and can be sampled as part of a *mezza,* or "combination" platter, which also features cucumbers, tomatoes, black olives and salty Syrian cheese. Nor should you miss the *safsouf* (cracked wheat-tomato-onion salad), its dressing fragrant with lemon juice, mint and parsley.

Preferred main courses include a well-charred shish kebab and *kibbie,* a sort of Middle East meatloaf made with cracked wheat and ground lamb. *Kufta,* a similar dish, features ground lamb meatballs seasoned with mint leaves. Nadia's stuffed cabbage leaves are good but the lemony stuffed grape leaves are better. I also like the Oriental-style chicken baked with rice, pignole nuts and cinnamon.

The house dessert is *baklava,* a sugar syrup-soaked cake made with ground nuts and thin, crisp sheets of filo dough. (In Greek, the word *filo* means "leaf.") Another plus: in the summer Nadia's serves iced coffee.

This friendly storefront has a color scheme typical of many Middle Eastern restaurants: red curtains, red tablecloths and red belly-dance tapestry on the paneled walls. A favorite haunt for night owls, Nadia's doesn't start hopping until 9 or 10 p.m. The juke box lists Arabic tunes on the left side and Western tunes on the right. True to the assimilation process, the Lebanese staff play the latter and avoid the former! Brown-bagging is not only tolerated but expected.

NEWBRIDGE CAFE

Rating: ★½

Type of cuisine: Italo-American barbecue

Price range: cheap

650 Washington Ave., Chelsea

Telephone: 884–0134

Hours: open Monday–Saturday from 11 a.m.–11 p.m.; Sunday from 1–10 p.m.

No reservations

No credit cards

Full bar

Wheelchair access adequate

Dress: casual

You would never guess from its bland exterior why this neighborhood lounge draws a loyal following from far beyond its surrounding Chelsea. Nor does the "dining room" with its black and red Naugahyde, blaring TV, and portraits of Elvis augur well for gastronomic attractions. It is not until the ship's bell by the kitchen clangs to announce that your food is ready and your waitress (somewhat more demure than those at Durgin-Park) bangs down a plate piled high with dinner, that you begin to understand the reason why the Newbridge Café is perennially packed with customers.

Any place that puts two cherrystones in a single half shell has the right idea about giving you your money's worth. (True, such largesse makes you question whether the bivalves were freshly shucked.) And if you don't mind sweet salad dressing, you could make a whole meal of the antipasto, a mountain of iceberg lettuce carpeted with provolone, *capacolla* (spicy shoulder ham), and other Italian cold cuts. But the real house specialty is the barbecued fare: moist, grilled lamb, Italian sausage loaded with pepper and fennel seed, and barbecued ribs so generous and meaty that you wonder whether or not they are pork chops. Entrees are accompanied by pickled peppers and enormous steak fries (the latter previously frozen). For dessert you have to go elsewhere.

As you'd expect at a neighborhood bar and grill, the Newbridge Café is extremely casual. Customers are apt to sport T-shirts and beer bellies and arrive in such numbers that a 45-minute wait for a table is typical on a Friday or Saturday night. Dinner music emanates from a juke box and "Mack the Knife," sung by Bobby Darin, is a house favorite.

NO NAME RESTAURANT

Rating: ★★

Type of cuisine: seafood

Price range: entrees from $4.50–8.00

15-½ Fish Pier, Boston

Telephone: 338–7539

Hours: open Monday–Saturday from 11 a.m.–10 p.m.

No reservations

No credit cards

BYOB

Wheelchair access difficult

Dress: casual

Proximity to the waterfront is no guarantee that a restaurant will serve great seafood, but an oceanside view does make decent fish taste all that much fresher. You can't get much closer to fresh fish, or the water, than at the No Name restaurant, sandwiched between packing houses on Boston's Fish Pier. Over the years, this Greek-run luncheonette has expanded to a one hundred-plus-seat fish house, acquiring a national reputation in the process. The perennially long waiting lines attest to No Name's popularity among both tourists and locals (the latter a youngish crowd). There are, of course, worse places to stand around drinking on a warm, midsummer eve than the cobblestoned Fish Pier with its superlative view of the harbor.

The virtue of No Name's bill of fare lies in its simplicity: impeccably fresh fish, broiled or crisply fried, without the gummy sauces with which so many restaurants slather their seafood in the name of gastronomic pretension. No Name's moist Boston scrod wears paprika, not the usual carpet of bread crumbs; bay scallops here come 40 to an order, nicely browned with butter. Broiled fish, like the salmon steaks, can be a bit dry, although you certainly can't quibble with the prodigious size of the portions. The house chowder is a no-nonsense soup free of potatoes and starchy thickeners. (Chowder, by the way, takes its name from the French *chaudière* or "cauldron" in which the early Breton settlers of Canada simmered their fish soups.) The fried clams (whole bivalves, not dry clam strips) are sensuously squishy in the center. The No Name even serves a dish of culinary pretension, mussels sauté, steamed open in wine and broiled with garlic butter.

The creamy coleslaw (Dutch "cabbage salad," brought to the U.S. first by settlers of "New Holland") is homemade. So is the pickle-studded tartar sauce and if the French fries taste previously frozen, the homemade blueberry and strawberry-rhubarb pies à la mode make up for them.

The No Name conforms to the low-life image of Boston fish houses with its appointments of garish fishing scenes, ship's lanterns, and long, communal tables serviced by shouting Greek waiters. Single diners or small parties can avoid the long waiting line by eating at the luncheonette counter: proceed directly to the entryway and turn right. The newly built rear dining room boasts a pretty harborside view through its wall-sized windows—tell the host you are willing to wait for a table there. After dinner you can stroll round the Fish Pier, where the wharf rats and stray fish carcasses may offend the faint-hearted, but the view of downtown Boston across the harbor is unsurpassed.

OCCASIONAL TABLE

Rating: ★½

Type of cuisine: health food breakfasts, lunchtime salads and sandwiches

Price range: cheap

398 Harvard St., Brookline

Telephone: 566–1771

Hours: open Tuesday–Saturday from 6 a.m.–4 p.m., Saturday and Sunday from 8 a.m.–4 p.m.

No reservations

No credit cards

BYOB

Wheelchair access good

Dress: casual

This New Age luncheonette makes the best chocolate chip cookies I have ever tasted, but dessert is just one reason for patronizing the Occasional Table. Located on the site of the former Sunnybrook Farms Deli, the Occasional Table draws a youngish crowd for its imaginative sandwiches and healthy breakfasts, the latter featuring huge fruit salads, moist bran muffins, and whole wheat pancakes and waffles. Occasional omelettes come with offbeat fillings, including boursin cheese with tomatoes or apples with tangy prosciutto. Sandwiches sound a health food theme, ranging from "Priscilla's peanut butter" (on whole wheat bread with bananas and honey) to "Uncle Jack's" (a variation on a grilled cheese sandwich made with Jarlsberg cheese and prosciutto). But my favorite is the *saucisson,* a hollowed out, crisply baked French roll stuffed with freshly cooked spinach and sausage.

The dining area has two conventional tables in the front window plus two communal tables fitted with low stools in the back. Counter service is also available. Good smells waft from the open kitchen which occupies half of the restaurant. The whitewashed walls are hung with artsy black and white photographs. Recorded music is provided by the likes of Stevie Wonder. The one thing I am not crazy about is the disposable plastic plates on which the food is served.

OH CALCUTTA

Rating: ★★

Type of cuisine: Indian

Price range: appetizers $1.50–3.00; entrees $4.00–7.00

468 Mass. Ave., Cambridge

Telephone: 576-2111

Hours: open seven days a week for lunch from 11 a.m.–3 p.m.; for dinner from 5–11 p.m.

No reservations

No credit cards

BYOB

Wheelchair access good

Dress: casual

Is Central Square about to become the new Bombay of Cambridge? So it would appear because two new Indian restaurants have recently joined the venerable India Pavillion and transformed this colorful neighborhood into a hotbed of Indian delights. I'm not quite sure what New Delhi-born Ascharj Gaggi had in mind when he named his restaurant Oh Calcutta, but the only thing indecent about this place I can see is its uncommonly low prices.

Calcutta appetizers sound a deep-fried theme, ranging from *pakoras* (shredded vegetable-chickpea batter fritters) to *alu tikka* (moist, mildly spiced potato croquettes). The *rikki tikki tavi* wins the ingenuity award, consisting of white bread balls stuffed with curried potatoes. All fried fare is served with tart tamarind sauce (made from a small brown fruit), plus fiery onion chutney. Other starters include *chat indira* (coriander-spiced fruit salad) and a perfumy coconut soup that might just as well be served at the end of a meal as at the beginning.

Pyromaniacs should order the lamb *vindaloo*, beneath whose chili hellfire lie lime juice, cinnamon, and ginger. The chicken *tikka* (marinated with yogurt, turmeric, and other spices) is equally delicious, but some of the curry dishes can be greasy. Indian desserts defy classification—my favorites include *ras malai* (fresh curd balls doused with rosewater-scented syrup) and *kheer* (cardamom-scented rice pudding). *Barfee* may not be the most inviting name for what the menu describes as "Indian brownie," but this nut-studded carrot cake is delicious. Although Oh Calcutta does not serve beer, the *lassi* (a rosewater-scented yogurt beverage) works well to extinguish the fires.

The no-frills dining room has seats for 50 on red plastic banquettes at white formica tables. The ministrations of the affable owner make up for the lack of the distinction of the decor. Wine or, more appropriately, beer can be purchased at Libby's Liquors across the street.

PAK NIN

Rating: ★★½

Type of cuisine: Chinese (Cantonese)

Price range: entrees $3.50–20.00 (most $5.00–6.00)

84 Harrison St., Boston

Telephone: 482–6168

Hours: open seven days a week from 11 a.m.–1 p.m.

Reservations accepted—usually not necessary

No credit cards

BYOB

Wheelchair access fair

Dress: casual

Habituées of New York's or San Francisco's Chinatown recognize the best restaurants by the colorful paper pennons festooning the walls that are covered with Chinese script describing the daily specials. Boston's Chinatown has one such restaurant, a place that the few Westerners who know about it mention in the conspiratorial whispers reserved for establishments whose whereabouts they would prefer not to disclose. Pak Nin's barebones dining room may be as undistinguished as its Garment District location, but I doubt you will find better Hong Kong-style cooking anywhere else in Chinatown.

Pak nin means "long life" in Chinese, and a steady diet of such house specialties as steak *kew*, crab with scallion and ginger, and salt baked chicken (marinated in wine and cooked in a salt crust) will insure a happy life if not an eternal one. For customers who don't read Chinese, the daily specials are listed in English on the first page of the menu. On recent visits, I have particularly enjoyed the watercress with shrimp sauce, roast squab (it tastes like a cross between duck and chicken), and frog legs with tangy black beans, the portion so huge it would constitute four servings at a typical French restaurant. In general, Pak Nin's prices are low (where else can you order a whole lobster with ginger sauce for $7.00?), but big spenders can treat themselves to such extravagances as steamed chicken with ham and vegetable greens ($19.00) and shark-fin-bird's-nest-chicken soup ($32.00 for two). One word of caution: the cooking is strictly authentic here, so some dishes, like the braised beef or green beans with pork, contain more fat than most Westerners feel comfortable eating.

Pak Nin's grey paneled walls bear little more decoration than the colorful pennons listing the daily specials. Guests sit at brown formica tables and are served by waiters who are atypically friendly for Chinatown. Children are welcomed here, too.

PLOUGH AND STARS

Rating: ★★

Type of cuisine: peasant

Price range: cheap

923 Massachusetts Ave., Cambridge

Telephone: 492–9653

Hours: lunch served Monday–Friday from noon–2:30 p.m.; Sunday brunch served from 1–4 p.m.

No reservations

No credit cards

Full bar

Wheelchair access good

Entertainment: live entertainment at night

Dress: casual

The Plough and Stars is the last place you would expect to find a well-heeled epicure, unless the epicure happened to like Guinness stout or Irish whiskey served in two-fisted tumblers amid tumult that makes a Celtic's game seem tranquil. At night, the "Plough," as it's affectionately called by regulars, is a hard-drinking Irish pub where the conversation often roars louder than the amplified jazz and Irish folk music usually featured.

By day, the Plough draws a more soft-spoken crowd of writers, artists, and other Cambridge denizens who repair here for lunch prepared by one

Mary Stackpole-Hayes, a self-taught chef who trained with an excellent teacher. For ten years now, Mary has served highly personal renditions of such international peasant classics as lamb curry with chutney, beef *en daube*, linguini with clams, mussels, and white sauce, and a unique chicken bouillabaisse. The Plough lunch includes French bread and butter and a salad made with Romaine lettuce instead of the usual iceberg. Best of all is that the lunch tab rarely exceeds $4. Rib-sticking soups and huge chef's salads are also served daily and on Sundays, a colorful, copious brunch is featured.

The Plough, with its polished wooden bar, red checkered table-cloths, and mirrored walls running the length of the narrow tavern, makes a cozy, homey, friendly neighborhood lunch spot.

ROSIE'S BAKERY AND DESSERT SHOP

Rating: ★★½

Type of cuisine: sweets and pastries (chocolate a house specialty)

Price range: cheap

243 Hampshire St., Cambridge

Telephone: 491–9488

9 Boylston St. (the Chestnut Hill Mall), Chestnut Hill

Hours: open Monday–Saturday from noon–midnight; Sunday from 10 a.m.–midnight

No reservations

No credit cards

No liquor

Wheelchair access tricky

Dress: casual

It's a good thing that Rosie's Bakery is only open daily from noon to midnight. Imagine how obese we would all be if her buttery congo bars or two-fisted oatmeal cookies were available every time we got the wee-hours munchies! For over half a decade, Rosie's has supplied area sweet-tooths with their sugar fix and I believe it is high time to reveal the identity of the woman behind the scene.

The real "Rosie" is one Judy Winograd, a former Museum Art School student who decided to decorate cookies for Valentine's Day one year and abruptly found herself in the pastry business. Operations soon overflowed her apartment kitchen to the family garage and from there to the tiny Inman Square storefront that Rosie's occupies today. (Incidentally, the author of this book served briefly as the baker at Rosie's predecessor, Legal's Sweet Shop). A few years ago, Judy's husband, Eliot, joined the business, describing himself as "a former mental health worker who now advocates sugar addiction." Together the Winograds have expanded their dessert empire all over greater Boston, supplying such establishments as Vie de France, the Harvard Bookstore Cafe, and the gourmet counter of a prestigious West Suburb department store that prefers to let its customers believe that the pastries are baked on the premises.

Chocoholics will have a religious experience with Rosie's fudgy cream cheese brownies and the incredibly rich, moist "chocolate orgasm" cake that fully lives up to its name. But to venture to Rosie's for chocolate alone would be to overlook an admirable cheesecake, a daily changing pound cake, and the crunchiest, most buttery shortbread this side of Scotland. Should your sugar craving be such that you can't wait to eat your dessert at home, you will find tables and white wire chairs for 16 in a postage-stamp-sized dining area decorated with pink ribbons, crocheted doilies, hanging plants, Rosie's T-shirts, and a wall plastered with an impressive selection of awards bestowed on Rosie's by the media. A second Rosie's is scheduled to open soon in the Chestnut Hill Mall. Both locations will sell home-baked croissants on Sundays.

RUBIN'S KOSHER DELICATESSEN AND RESTAURANT

Rating: ★★½

Type of cuisine: kosher

Price range: entrees $3.50–7.50

500 Harvard St., Brookline

Telephone: 566–8761

Hours: open Monday–Thursday from 9 a.m.–8 p.m.; Friday from 8 a.m.–3 p.m.; Sunday from 8 a.m.–8 p.m.; closed Saturdays and during Passover

No reservations

No credit cards

No liquor

Wheelchair access good

Dress: casual

Rubin's is the one Brookline deli where you *won't* find bagels and cream cheese. For over half a century, Rubin's has reigned as Boston's foremost, and today only, fully kosher restaurant and, as the *kashrut* (Jewish dietary code) strictly forbids combining meat with dairy products, no milk (only coffee-lite), no butter (only margarine), and no cream cheese (not even with smoked fish) are served here. Not that Rubin's customers feel deprived—not by a long shot—because the well-heaped sandwiches require both hands for lifting and the generous deli platters could have come right out of the wedding scene of *Goodbye, Columbus.*

What distinguishes Rubin's from the other kosher-style restaurants in Brookline? "Our secret is that we cook all our own tongue, brisket, and corned beef right on the premises," says proprietor Larry Grupp, whose grandfather and uncle opened a kosher delicatessen and catering service in Brookline in the 30's. Rubin's lunch meats, like the renowned, thick-sliced Roumanian pastrami, are imported directly from New York and are warmed not in a microwave but on an old-fashioned steam table for extra moistness. The homemade *kishka* (beef gut filled with bread stuffing) comes with real brisket gravy and the *kugel* (noodle pudding) is as thick as the Boston yellow pages.

Other Jewish specialties here include stuffed cabbage, homemade *tzimas* (sweet stewed carrots and onions), and a chopped liver that's as flavorful as my grandmother's own. And to wash your meal down there are two kinds of cream soda, not to mention Cel-Ray, a celery-flavored soda that is a natural with delicatessen fare.

In 1979, Rubin's moved from its original location at 400 Harvard St. to the modern building it occupies presently. The red and silver wallpaper and booths with red Naugahyde banquets and formica tabletops don't necessarily fit my image of what a traditional kosher deli should look like but, then again, the waitresses in their black skirts and ruffled white blouses are as kindly as Jewish grandmothers. In the unlikely event that you leave Rubin's hungry, your snack needs will be more than amply met at the carry-out counter to the right of the dining area.

TOSCANINI'S

Rating: ★★

Type of cuisine: ice cream

Price range: cheap

899 Main St., Cambridge

Telephone: 491–5877

Hours:

No reservations

No credit cards

No liquor

Wheelchair access fair

Dress: casual

According to a recent survey by a prominent New York PR firm, New Englanders have the highest per capita consumption of ice cream in the nation, a whopping 21.86 quarts a year! That fact probably comes as no surprise to most Bostonians, who have long been blessed with a multitude of ice cream parlors specializing in freshly churned ice cream and sherbet. Opened in November, 1980, Toscanini's may be a newcomer to the Boston ice cream scene but already this boutique parlor has captured a citywide audience for such audacious flavors as kiwi-banana, ginger-snap-molasses, and, believe it or not, avocado.

Toscanini owners Gus Rancatore and Kurt Jaenicke make all their ice cream in an old-fashioned ice and salt churn in the window, using fresh fruits, real liquors, and ground-up cookies. Their vanilla received this critic's vote in an ice cream contest conducted by *Boston Magazine*. On any given day there are eight flavors to choose from, including a chocolate hazelnut, lemon honey, and an ice cream flavored with Postum.

Mix-ins are available here as are sundaes topped with homemade sauces, like the unusual hot mint fudge.

Located near MIT, Toscanini's does a lively carry-out trade but there are circus chairs and white wire tables (and a supply of newspapers to read) for people who wish to get their licks on the premises. Another plus, the staff plies you with samples to help you select your flavor.

WILLOW POND KITCHEN

Rating: ★½

Type of cuisine: American/seafood

Price range: entrees $4.00–7.00

Route 2A in Concord

No telephone

Hours: open Monday–Saturday 11 a.m.–11 p.m.; Sunday from 1–11 p.m.

No reservations

No credit cards

Beer and wine

Wheelchair access good

Dress: casual

The "Willow," as it is called by the locals, may be a mere five-minute drive from the Bridge that Arched the Flood, but a distance greater than that of miles or centuries separates this boisterous roadhouse from the neat clapboard homes of historic Concord. There is nothing quaint about the Willow where pickup trucks kick up gravel in the parking lot and blue collar epicures devour hardy, inexpensive fare with gusto.

Willow owner Peter Sowkow serves a rib-sticking clam chowder (his corn chowder isn't bad, either), not to mention mountains of steamers (these can be gritty), fried clams, fried mussels, and even batter-fried frog legs. The real house specialty is lobster, however, and at this writing $7 will fetch you a 1-¼ pounder plus coleslaw, a dinner roll, and a moist, cheese-stuffed potato. Other popular items here are the pizza, steaks (remarkable for their low prices, if not their tenderness), and a character-istically bland boiled dinner. The billowy dinner rolls are homemade but avoid the store-bought pies when time comes for dessert.

The low slung dining room has lots of atmosphere. It is decorated with stuffed bobcats, World War I relics, and wooden booths framed by red checkered curtains. Dinner "music" is provided by a color TV over the bar. The waitresses are brusque but friendly—a suburban version of the staff at Durgin-Park.

WOODMAN'S

Rating: ★½

Type of cuisine: seafood (fried clams are the house specialty)

Price range: cheap

Main St. (Route 133), Essex

Telephone: 768–6451

Hours: open from 11:30 a.m.–10 p.m. seven days a week

No reservations

No credit cards

Full bar

Wheelchair access good

Dress: casual

City fathers seldom erect statues to honor great chefs or their creations. If this were not so, surely the town of Essex would have raised a monument in front of the boisterous fish house on Main St. to honor a most famous Bay State citizen, Lawrence Woodman. On this spot, on July 3, 1916, the owner of a tiny refreshment stand that would henceforth bear his name shucked, battered, and deep-fried an Ipswich bivalve. Thus was born that renowned New England delicacy: the fried clam.

Fried clams remain the house specialty of Woodman's but not the only specialty. The open kitchen, with its Dante-esque bank of friolators, also doles out delicious steamers, clam cakes, chowder, and fish and chip platters. Live lobsters are fished from a pool in front of the "restaurant" to be steamed over a brick oven and served on cardboard plates. Side dishes may be few in number but the coleslaw has a sourish tang that lets you know it's homemade and the freshly fried onion rings are so crisp they crackle like corn doodles when you bite into them.

The management, now into the third generation of Woodmans, isn't kidding when it describes a meal at Woodman's as "eating in the rough." There are no waitresses—you queue up in one line to place and pay for your order and in a second line to purchase beer or liquor. Your number will be called when your order is ready; should you desire tartar sauce or melted butter, you have to pay for it separately. Worn formica tables with church pew benches crowd the noisy "dining" area. You can escape the commotion (and watch seagulls wheel overhead) by carrying your food to one of the less than immaculate picnic tables out back.

II

I'M IN THE MOOD FOR . . .

CROSS-REFERENCES

Part II is a comprehensive cross-reference that tells you where to find whatever sort of food, setting, or dining experience you desire. Below are listed the categories with an explanation when necessary.

American

Central European

Chinese (Cantonese)—The mild traditional cooking of southeast China. Typical flavors include soy sauce, rice wine, scallion, ginger, and black beans (tangy fermented soy beans).

Chinese (Szechuan/Mandarin)—Szechuan is a south central Chinese cooking style distinguished by its lavish use of sesame oil and chili peppers. Mandarin refers to a pan-national cuisine designed for the wealthy Mandarin class of government officials.

Chinese (*dim sum*)—Chinese "snacks" or tea pastries served from 10 a.m.–3 p.m.

Contemporary—sometimes described as "the new American cooking" or "American *nouvelle cuisine.*" Expect striking plate presentations, unusual flavor combinations (including fruit vinegars, nut oils, smoked foods, and arcane salad greens), and starchless reduction sauces (made by boiling down wine, cream, and stock to obtain intense, buttery sauces). Contemporary restaurants serve truly international menus, with French, Northern Italian, and even Oriental influences in evidence.

Continental—describes the Franco-Italo-American food served at many hotel restaurants

Delicatessen

French

Health Food—not necessarily vegetarian, but many non-meat dishes served

Iberian

Indian

Italian—describes the robust, tomato-based cooking of Southern Italy and Italian neighborhoods in this country.

Italian (Northern)—refers to a more delicate, low tomato cuisine based on homemade pasta, cream sauces, and unusual ingredients like extra virgin olive oil, arugula (a peppery salad green), and sun-dried tomatoes.

Japanese

Latin American—includes Brazilian, Cuban, and Mexican

Middle East/Greek

Miscellaneous Ethnic—includes Burmese, Ethiopian, and Korean

Nouvelle Cuisine—like "Contemporary," only French

Peasant

Seafood

Steak

Thai

(Please note that when stars are listed in this sub-section, they apply to the particular category (e.g.... breakfast or spectacular setting), not the overall rating of the restaurant, which is found in Part I.)

Breakfast—(*note*: many of the places cited for breakfast also serve lunch and dinner)

Brunch—(*see note above*)

Coffee Houses and High Teas—(*see note above*)

Finger Food—ribs, sandwiches, burgers, etc.

Ice Cream and Cake

Spectacular Settings

Romantic Havens

Entertainment Nightly

History (places to take tourists)

Night Owl's Delight

Outdoor Terraces

Private Dining Rooms

By Location

Downtown Boston

Back Bay/South End/Kenmore Square

Brookline (Brighton/Allston)

Cambridge

Somerville

North of Boston

West of Boston

South of Boston

AMERICAN

Beetle's Lunch	$	★★
Bob the Chef (Soul Food)	$	★★
Brandy Pete's	$$	★★
Brookline Lunch	$	★★
Charlie's Sandwich Shoppe	$	★★
Durgin-Park	$–$$	★★½
Harvard Do-nut Shop	$	★½
Hoodoo Barbecue	$	★★½
Locke-Ober Café	$$$	★★★½
Newbridge Café (Ribs)	$	★½
Occasional Table	$	★½
Willow Pond Kitchen	$	★½

CENTRAL EUROPEAN

Cafe Budapest	$$$	★★★

CHINESE (Cantonese)

Carl's Pagoda	$$	★★½
Ho Yuen Ting	$	★★½
Imperial Teahouse	$–$$	★★
Moon Villa	$–$$	★★
Pak Nin	$	★★½

CHINESE (Szechuan/Mandarin)

Chef Chang's House	$	★★
Chang Feng	$	★★
Imperial Teahouse	$–$$	★★
Mandalay	$–$$	★★★
Mary Chung	$	★★½

CHINESE (*Dim Sum*)

Imperial Teahouse	$–$$	★★½
Mary Chung	$	★★½
Moon Villa	$–$$	★★

CONTEMPORARY

Another Season	$$$	★★★
Apley's	$$$	★★★★
Blue Strawbery	$$$	★★★

Café Calypso	$$	★★½
Chez Nous	$$–$$$	★★★
Cybele on Waterfront	$$–$$$	★★★
Harvard Bookstore Café	$–$$	★★
The Harvest Restaurant	$$$	★★★½
Icarus	$$$	★★★
Lenora	$$$	★★★
Panache	$$$	★★★★
St. Botolph Restaurant	$$–$$$	★★★
Seasons Restaurant	$$$	★★★½
Tigerlilies	$$	★★
29 Newbury St.	$$	★★★
Voyagers	$$$	★★★

CONTINENTAL

Another Season	$$$	★★★
Bay Tower Room	$$$	★★
Café Plaza	$$$	★★★
Cybele on the Waterfront	$$–$$$	★★★
Locke-Ober Café	$$$	★★★½
Mill Falls	$$$	★★
Ritz-Carlton	$$$	★★★

DELICATESSEN

| B and D Deli | $ | ★★ |
| Rubin's | $ | ★★½ |

FRENCH

Chillingsworth	$$$	★★★★
Julien at Hotel Meridien	$$$	★★★½
L'Espalier	$$$	★★★★
Maison Robert	$$$	★★
Voyagers	$$$	★★★

HEALTH FOOD

Seventh Inn	$$	★★½
Last Chance Café	$	★½
Annapurna	$	★★½
Bel Canto	$	★★

IBERIAN

O Fado	$–$$	★★½
Sol Posto	$$	★★

INDIAN

Annapurna	$	★★½
Kebab-N-Kurry	$	★★½
Oh Calcutta	$	★★

ITALIAN

Sabatino's	$$	★★½
Bel Canto (pizza)	$	★★
Bertucci's Pizza and Bocce	$	★★
Caffe Paradiso	$	★★
Daily Catch	$–$$	★★½
Galeria Umberto	$	★★
Newbridge Café	$	★½

ITALIAN (Northern)

Allegro	$$$	★★★½
Upstairs at the Pudding	$$$	★★★½
La Primavera	$$	★★★

JAPANESE

Genji	$$	★★★
Tatsukichi-Boston	$$	★★★
Chieko	$	★★

LATIN AMERICAN

Sol Azteca	$$	★★★
Buteco	$	★★★
La Espagnola (Cuban)	$	★★

MIDDLE EAST/GREEK

Aegean Fare	$	★
Algiers Coffee House	$	★★
Nadia's Eastern Star	$	★★

MISCELLANEOUS ETHNIC

Mandalay (Burmese)	$–$$	★★★
Korea House (Korean)	$	★★½
Lalibela (Ethiopian)	$	★½

NOUVELLE CUISINE

Chez Nous	$$	★★★
Chillingsworth	$$$	★★★★
Julien at Hotel Meridien	$$$	★★★½
L'Espalier	$$$	★★★★
Panache	$$$	★★★★

PEASANT

Peasant Stock	$$	★★
Plough and Stars	$	★★

SEAFOOD

Anthony's Pier 4	$$	★★
Legal Sea Foods	$$	★★★
The Mass. Bay Co.	$$	★★★
No Name Restaurant	$	★★
Daily Catch	$–$$	★★½
Willow Pond Kitchen	$	★½
Woodman's	$	★½

STEAK

Callahan's	$$	★★½
Grill 23	$$–$$$	★★★
Hilltop Steak House	$–$$	★½
Newbury Steak House	$–$$	★★
Scotch 'N Sirloin	$$	★★

THAI

Bangkok Cuisine	$–$$	★★½
Thai Cuisine	$–$$	★★½

(Note: Stars apply to particular category, not to overall restaurant rating.)

BREAKFAST

Café Plaza	$$	★★★★
Ritz-Carlton	$	★★★
Harvard Do-Nut Shop	$	★★★
B and D Deli	$	★★½
Beetle's Lunch	$	★★½
Brookline Lunch	$	★★½
Harvard Bookstore Café	$	★★
Charlie's Sandwich Shoppe	$	★★
Occasional Table	$	★½

BRUNCH

(*Note:* only restaurants with noteworthy brunches are listed)

Jonah's on the Terrace	$$	★★★★
Lenora	$$	★★★★
Cybele on the Waterfront	$$	★★★½
Imperial Teahouse	$	★★★½
Café Plaza (Copley's Restaurant)	$$	★★★
Chillingsworth	$$	★★★
The Harvest Restaurant	$$	★★★
Icarus	$$	★★★
Peasant Stock	$$	★★★
La Primavera	$$	★★★
St. Botolph	$$	★★★
Seasons Restaurant	$$	★★★
Beetle's Lunch	$	★★½
Café Calypso	$	★★½
Mary Chung (*dim sum*)	$	★★½
Plough and Stars	$	★★½

COFFEE HOUSES and HIGH TEAS

Coffee Connection	$	★★★★
Café Plaza (tea)	$	★★★★
Ritz-Carlton (tea)	$	★★★★
Algiers Coffee House	$	★★★★
Caffé Paradiso	$	★★½

| Harvard Bookstore Café | $ | ★★½ |
| Harvard Do-Nut Shop | $ | ★½ |

FINGER FOOD

Galeria Umberto	$	★★★★
Hoodoo Barbecue (ribs)	$	★★★★
Rubin's (sandwiches)	$	★★★★
Bel Canto (pizza)	$	★★★
Bertucci's Pizza and Bocce	$	★★★
Harvard Do-Nut Shop (muffins)	$	★★★
Lalibela (Ethiopian—you eat with your fingers)	$	★★★
Woodman's (fried clams)	$	★★★
Coffee Connection (sandwiches)	$	★★½
Harvard Bookstore Cafe (sandwiches)	$	★★½
Occasional Table (sandwiches)	$	★★½
B and D Deli (sandwiches)	$	★★
Newbridge Café (ribs)	$	★★
Charlie's Sandwich Shoppe	$	★½

ICE CREAM AND CAKE

Ice Cream
Joey's	$	★★★★
Herrell's	$	★★★½
Caffe Paradiso	$	★★½
Toscanini's	$	★★½

Cake
Rosie's	$	★★★★
Coffee Connection	$	★★★½
Harvard Bookstore Café	$	★★★

SPECTACULAR SETTINGS

Bay Tower Room	$$$	★★★★
Voyagers (upstairs)	$$$	★★★★
Café Plaza	$$$	★★★½
Julien at Hotel Meridien	$$$	★★★½
L'Espalier	$$$	★★★½
Ritz-Carlton	$$$	★★★½

Chillingsworth	$$$	★★★
Maison Robert (upstairs)	$$$	★★★
Mill Falls	$$$	★★★
Tigerlilies	$$	★★★
Seasons Restaurant	$$$	★★½
Cybele on the Waterfront	$$	★★
Jonah's on the Terrace (seats near window only)	$$	★★
Lenora	$$$	★★
St. Botolph	$$	★★
Aegean Fare	$	★½
Anthony's Pier 4 (seats near water only)	$$	★½

ROMANTIC HAVENS

Another Season	$$$	★★★★
Bay Tower Room	$$$	★★★★
Voyagers	$$$	★★★★
Café Budapest (lounge & "Blue Room")	$$$	★★★
Chez Nous	$$	★★★
Chillingsworth ("proposal room")	$$$	★★★
L'Espalier	$$$	★★★
Icarus	$$$	★★

ENTERTAINMENT NIGHTLY

Bay Tower Room (orchestra & dance floor)	$$$	★★★★
Peasant Stock (music & drama)	$$	★★★★
Café Budapest (piano & violin in lounge)	$$$	★★★
Voyagers (harp and/or harpsicord)	$$$	★★★
Apley's (classical guitar & harp)	$$$	★★
Bertucci's Pizza and Bocce (bocce ball)	$	★★
Café Plaza (piano)	$$$	★★
Harvard Bookstore Café (good reading)	$$	★★
Jonah's on the Terrace (chamber music)	$$	★★
Julien at Hotel Meridien (piano, dancing in the Café Fleuri)	$$$	★★
O Fado (Portuguese folk music & dancing)	$	★★

Plough and Stars (live jazz & Irish music at night)	$	★★
Scotch 'N Sirloin (live & taped dance music in lounge)	$$	★★
Sol Azteca (guitar)	$$	★★
Mill Falls (piano in lounge)	$$$	★½
Ritz-Carlton (piano)	$$$	★½
Sol Posto (The Sunset Café) (Portuguese music)	$	★

HISTORY (places to take tourists)

Durgin-Park (Faneuil Hall as it was 100 years ago)	$	★★★★
Locke-Ober Café (museum quality Gay Nineties decor)	$$$	★★★★
Anthony's Pier 4 (not old despite the pseudo-colonial garb of the wait staff— but certainly a Boston institution!)	$$	★★★
Chillingsworth (a 17th century mansion filled with antiques)	$$$	★★★
Brandy Pete's (a vintage business district lunchroom)	$$	★★
Charlie's Sandwich Shoppe (the Big Band greats dined here, and so can you!)	$	★★
Julien (located in the members court of of the old Federal Reserve Building)	$$$	★½
Maison Robert (located in Old City Hall— Boston's best surviving example of Second Empire architecture)	$$$	★½

NIGHT OWL'S DELIGHT

Aegean Fare (till 4 a.m.)
Moon Villa (till 4 a.m.)
Scotch 'N Sirloin (lounge open till 2 a.m. on weekends; kitchen closes at 11:30 p.m.)
Coffee Connection (till 1 a.m. on weekends)

Imperial Tea House (till 1 a.m.)
Nadia's Eastern Star (till 1 a.m.)

OUTDOOR TERRACES

Maison Robert	$$$	★★★★
Mill Falls	$$$	★★★★
Tigerlilies	$$	★★★★
Voyagers (indoor greenhouse)	$$$	★★★★
Anthony's Pier 4	$$	★★★
Chez Nous	$$	★★★
Chillingsworth	$$$	★★★
The Harvest Restaurant	$$–$$$	★★★
29 Newbury Street	$$	★★★
Harvard Bookstore Cafe	$$	★★½
La Primavera	$$	★★½
Algiers Coffee House	$	★★

PRIVATE DINING ROOMS

Bay Tower Room	$$$	★★★★
Café Plaza	$$$	★★★
Chillingsworth	$$$	★★★
Cybele on the Waterfront	$$	★★★
Locke-Ober Café	$$$	★★★
Maison Robert	$$$	★★★
Ritz-Carlton	$$$	★★★
Anthony's Pier 4	$$	★★
Genji	$$	★★
The Harvest Restaurant	$$$	★★
Tatsukichi-Boston	$$	★★

RESTAURANTS BY LOCATION
Downtown Boston
$$$

Another Season (Beacon Hill)	★★★
Bay Tower Room	★★
Julien at the Hotel Meridien	★★★½
Locke-Ober Café	★★★

Maison Robert	★★
Seasons Restaurant (Quincy Market area)	★★★½

$$

Anthony's Pier 4	★★
Brandy Pete's	★★
Carl's Pagoda (Chinatown)	★★½
Cybele on the Waterfront	★★★
Sabatino's (North End)	★★½
Scotch 'N Sirloin	★★
Tatsukichi-Boston (Quincy Market Area)	★★★
Tigerlilies (Beacon Hill)	★★

$

Buteco (Fenway)	★★★
Caffe Paradiso (North End)	★★
Daily Catch (North End)	★★½
Durgin-Park (Quincy Market area)	★★
Galeria Umberto (North End)	★★
Imperial Teahouse (Chinatown)	★★
La Espagnola (Jamaica Plain)	★★
Pak Nin (Chinatown)	★★½

Back Bay/Kenmore Square (K)/South End (S)
$$$

Apley's	★★★★
Café Budapest	★★★
Café Plaza	★★★
Icarus (S)	★★★
L'Espalier	★★★★
Ritz-Carlton	★★★

$$

Bangkok Cuisine	★★½
Café Calypso (S)	★★½
Genji	★★★

$$

Grill 23	★★★
Harvard Bookstore Café	★★½
Legal Sea Foods	★★★
Mass. Bay Co.	★★★
Newbury Steak House	★★
St. Botolph (S)	★★★
Seventh Inn	★★½
Thai Cuisine	★★½
29 Newbury St.	★★★

$

Aegean Fare (K)	★
Bob the Chef (S)	★★
Charlie's Sandwich Shoppe (S)	★★
Hoodoo Barbecue (K)	★★½
Kebab 'N' Kurry	★★½
Lalibela	★½
Mandalay	★★★
Nadia's Eastern Star (S)	★★

Brookline (Brighton/Allston)
$$

Chef Chang's House	★★
Sol Azteca	★★★

$

B and D Deli	★★
Beetle's Lunch	★★
Occasional Table	★½

Cambridge
$$$

Harvest	★★★½
Lenora	★★★

Panache	★★★★
Upstairs at the Pudding	★★★½
Voyagers	★★★

$$

Chez Nous	★★★
Jonah's on the Terrace	★★½
Legal Sea Foods	★★★
Peasant Stock	★★
La Primavera	★★★
Sol Posto	★★

$

Algiers Coffee House	★★½
Bel Canto	★★
Brookline Lunch	★★
Coffee Connection	★★½
Harvard Do-Nut Shop	★½
Herrell's	★★
Korea House	★★½
Last Chance Café	★½
Mary Chung	★★½
Plough and Stars	★★
Rosie's Bakery	★★½
Toscanini's	★★

Somerville
$

Bel Canto	★★
Bertucci's Pizza and Bocce	★★
Chang Feng	★★
Chieko	★★
Joey's	★★½

North of Boston
$$$

Blue Strawbery (Portsmouth, New Hampshire)	★★★

O Fado (Peabody)	★★½
Hilltop Steak House (Saugus)	★½
Newbridge Café (Chelsea)	★½
Woodman's (Essex)	★½

West of Boston
$$$

Allegro (Waltham)	★★★½
Mill Falls (Upper Newton Falls)	★★

$$

Callahan's (Newton/Wayland)	★★½
Legal Sea Foods (Chestnut Hill)	★★★

$

Annapurna (Worcester)	★★½
Willow Pond Kitchen (Concord)	★½

South of Boston
$$$

Chillingsworth	★★★★

III

SECRETS OF A RESTAURANT CRITIC

A BRIEF RESTAURANT ETIQUETTE GUIDE FOR DINNER GUESTS AND WAITERS

The quality of any dining experience depends not only on the food but also on setting and service. Good service can go a long way toward making a poor meal palatable, while bad service can spoil the efforts of the very best chef. The job of any waiter or waitress is to provide prompt, courteous service, but the dinner guest also has responsibilities for making a meal flow smoothly. Below are a few ways you can help to ensure better service, as well as some advice on what to do when you don't get the meal you ordered.

Reservations: Boston is a dine-out city and, on the weekends, reservations are a must at all better restaurants. When possible, book your table at least two weeks ahead of time. Arrive on time (or a few minutes early) for your reservation or, if you know you are going to be late, call the restaurant to warn them. (The restaurant will appreciate the courtesy and it may prevent the maitre d' from giving your table to someone else.) If your party of four grows to five, or shrinks to three, let the restaurant know: good restaurants have tables designed for a specific number of people and adding or subtracting a place setting at the last minute is never as comfortable as getting the right-sized table at the outset. If, for some reason, you are unable to honor your reservation, cancel it as early as possible.

It is grossly inconsiderate to make reservations at more than one restaurant for a particular evening. No-shows hurt all of us: the customer who had to dine elsewhere because he couldn't get a reservation; the restaurant owner who raises his prices to cover lost revenues; and other dinner guests, who are forced to wait in long lines on Saturday night because the restaurateur finally decided that it just wasn't profitable to accept reservations.

Avoid Rush Hour: When I want to experience a restaurant at its best, I make my reservations for a Wednesday or Thursday evening. A restaurant can't possibly show you its best at 8 p.m. on Saturday when the kitchen and serving staff are overburdened with capacity crowds. If you do dine out on the weekend, dine early (6 to 7 p.m.) or better still, dine late (9:30 p.m. or after). Having sped the 8 p.m. horde through their dinners, the staff will have the time to give you the individual attention you deserve.

Getting the Right Table: At my dream restaurant, every table would have the best seats in the house. In reality, this is not how it works, as some tables are invariably and unfortunately closer to the kitchen, restrooms, or entryway than others. If you have been to the restaurant beforehand, the best way to assure yourself of a good spot is to request a specific table when you make your reservations. If you don't like a particular table, say something to the maitre d' *before* you are seated. If you see a free table you prefer, ask for it; if you strongly dislike the only available table, offer to wait until another becomes available. Be firm, but be polite. Of course, you are the one who is paying for dinner but, at the same time, it does no good to incur the enmity of the person who will be waiting on you for the rest of the evening.

Single diners, especially single women diners, should not allow themselves to be intimidated into accepting an inferior table (although they might prefer the privacy of a seat in a corner or by the wall). I don't believe that receiving decent service or a good table should depend on greasing the palm of the captain. Nonetheless, if you plan to return to the restaurant, a token of your appreciation, slipped discreetly to the maitre d' *after* the meal, may help him to remember you in the future.

A note to restaurateurs: when the wait for a reserved table is excessive, most people would appreciate the courtesy of a complimentary cocktail.

What To Do About Slow or Rude Service: Slow service is not always the fault of the waiter. Behind the kitchen doors there occur a multitude of eleventh hour emergencies or untimely disasters. If the wait for an entree seems eternal, chances are the cook burned it or forgot to put it into the oven. The waiter is probably as chagrined as you are and harsh words serve only to put both of you in a bad humor.

A good waiter will warn you if a specific dish takes particularly long to prepare or if the kitchen is behind schedule. (I am much more apt to forgive a tardy entree when I have been forewarned.) If the waiter fails to say anything after a reasonable amount of time, ask politely about the status of your order. If you are not satisfied with the response, or if the delay continues longer than 20 minutes between the time the dishes of the previous course are cleared and the new ones are brought, ask to speak to the manager. If worse comes to worst, and you decide that dinner is simply not worth the wait, request the check and offer to pay for what you have already eaten. No restaurateur in his right mind would accept your money, but at least you had the courtesy to offer.

When dealing with waiters and waitresses, I try to be as compassionate as possible. After all, they have one of the world's most difficult jobs—pleasing a difficult public. Before you yell at a waiter or waitress, consider what it must be like to deal with temperamental chefs in infernal kitchen conditions. I find that sympathy goes a lot further than anger and that yelling serves chiefly to alienate your waiter (a potential ally) and upset you and your companions. There is something I won't tolerate on the part of a server, however; rudeness. There is only one thing to do when confronted with rude service: call for the manager and insist that you be given a different waiter.

Sending Food Back: There are three circumstances under which food should be sent back: when it is cold, improperly prepared, or is different from what you ordered. The first is the most easily remedied, tell your waiter that your dish is cold and that you would like the kitchen to rewarm it. (In most cases, another 60 seconds in the oven will bring the dish to the proper temperature.)

Improper preparation may include a hair in the soup, a fish that tastes spoiled, or a sauce that is oversalted. In the case of the bad fish, order another entree (preferably a non-fish one and something that can be prepared quickly). The chances are that if one piece of meat or fish tastes bad, others, too, will be suspect, if not actually tainted. In the case of under- or over-seasoning, particularly if you are at the sort of restaurant where each dish is prepared to order, you might try re-ordering the wayward dish in the hope that this time the chef will be more careful. What to do about a hair in the soup depends on how squeamish you are. You certainly are entitled to send it back, in which case I would order something different. In all but the best restaurants, I would simply fish it out; that is what the chef will do when you send it back, and there are probably more where that one came from, no matter what you order.

There are circumstances under which you should *not* send food back; not liking a dish you have not previously tried is foremost among them. It is not the restaurant's fault if sweetbreads taste differently than you thought they would; sending them back to the kitchen would be like returning a once-played record album because you didn't care for the music. (A good waiter will take notice if a customer leaves a dish untouched and many restaurants will offer to provide a replacement, free of charge.)

When sending food back, do so as soon as you have tasted the dish and there is still time to do something about it. Do not eat food you intend to send back. If I were a restaurateur and someone complained about a dish after he had cleaned his plate, I would not hesitate to charge them for it. I do not expect to be billed, however, for flawed food that I did not touch.

The Moment of Reckoning: A tip may once have been a token of appreciation bestowed upon a particularly capable or solicitous waiter. Today it should be considered as part of the fixed cost of a meal. Bostonians have a bad reputation for being chintzy tippers; here is what I recommend you tip.

Waiters or waitresses: 15 percent of the total tab (including drinks) for adequate service; 18 percent for good service; 20 percent for excellent service. (To calculate 15 percent, multiply the meal tax times 3; to calculate 20 percent, move the decimal point over one column to the left and multiply times 2.) I always tip 20 percent at an inexpensive restaurant —for an extra 50¢ you can feel like a big shot.

Maitre d': When a maitre d' does something special for you (prepares a salad, suggests a wine, reserves you a particularly nice table, etc.) tip him 5 percent of the total tab. If he does nothing other than show you to the table, you are not obliged to tip him. When a captain prepares your dinner at tableside and the waiter simply serves it, leave the captain 5–10 percent and reduce the waiter's tip accordingly.

Wine Steward: If the wine steward has been especially helpful or has spent a long time consulting with you on your wine selection, leave him $5 or 10 percent of the bar bill. If you order a particularly rare bottle of wine, it is a nice courtesy to offer him a glass or leave him 3 to 4 ounces of wine in the bottle.

Coat Check Person: $1 for four coats, or 50¢ per coat

Restroom Attendant: 50¢

Car Park Valet: $1

Note: these are minimums. Far be it from me to bridle your generosity should you want to give more.

When to Undertip or "Stiff" the Waiter: If the service has been discourteous or poor through the fault of the waiter, you are well within your rights to leave a 5–10 percent tip (perhaps he or she will get the message). If the service has been really terrible, you can leave the restaurant without tipping. The best restaurant revenge story was told to me by a caller when I was a guest on the Dick Syatt radio show. I hope this courageous woman is reading this book right now: "I was dining by myself at Restaurant X. The maitre d' gave me the worst seat in the house and throughout dinner the waiter was inexcusably rude. At the end of the meal I left a crisp $10 bill on the table and exited the restaurant without saying a word.

"The next evening, I returned to the restaurant. This time no table was good enough for the solitary diner and the waiter who had been so negligent the preceding evening hovered over me as though I were visiting royalty. At the end of the meal, I summoned him to the table, reached into my pocketbook, and placed two shiny pennies in his out-stretched palm. "This is for last night's dinner," I told him, "and the $10 bill was for tonight."

I trust that the waiter got the lady's point!

SEVEN STRATEGIES FOR GREAT CHEAP DINING

Nobody likes to spend more than necessary for dinner and, in these days of skyrocketing food prices, restaurant-goers cannot afford *not* to be thrifty. In the course of dining around Boston over the past six years, I have evolved some surefire methods for picking great low-price restaurants and for keeping the tab under control at expensive ones. Herewith are some strategies for great economical dining.

1. *Eat Ethnic:* The best food values are to be found at Boston's Latin, Middle East, and Oriental restaurants. Most ethnic chefs spend their money on the ingredients, not the decor, and the savings are passed on to the customers. Try to pick places where English is the second language; an ethnic clientele helps keep a kitchen staff honest.

2. *Seek Places With No Liquor License:* The average markup on wine at a restaurant is 200 to 300 percent. Brown bagging eliminates the bar tab while enabling you to drink good wine at reasonable prices. Restaurants with no liquor licenses do not automatically permit BYOB. You should call ahead to determine the current policy.

3. *Mind Your Ps and Qs:* In the 18th century barmaids used to record a tavern guest's bar tab in "pints" and "quarts." Restaurants still derive their highest profits from liquor sales (Think how many $3 martinis you can pour from a $10 bottle of gin.) Far be it from me to advocate abstinence, but one way to cut the cost of dining out is to skip cocktails and proceed directly to the wine. Once there, avoid "big name" wines like Chateau-Neuf-de-Pape and Pouilly-Fuisse where you pay for their snob appeal. The best wine values in France are from Alsace, the Loire Valley, and the Beaujolais. Among white California wines, sauvignon blancs tend to be more reasonably priced than chardonnays; for red, try a merlot or zinfandel instead of a costly cabernet sauvignon. But the best quaffs for the money are the wines from Italy, Spain (excellent for

cheap champagne), Portugal, and especially Eastern Europe (particularly Hungary and Roumania for reds).

Finally, don't overlook beer and ale. Either make an inexpensive, bone-dry beverage with Oriental, Latin, and Central European food.

4. *Eat at Off Hours:* If you want to try some of the pricier restaurants, lunch is usually less expensive than dinner and often the food is the same. Also, for people who enjoy restaurants for their setting, daylight dining allows better appreciation of architectural details. The same holds true for breakfast, a meal served with particular magnificence in the grand hotel dining rooms. Finally, many restaurants offer special discounts or two for the price of one specials at off hours (early evening) or on slow nights, like Monday, Tuesday, and Wednesday.

5. *Make a Meal of Appetizers:* Appetizers are usually the best part of the meal and at most restaurants you can order 3 to 4 appetizers for the price of a single entree. (Some restaurants discourage this practice so consult with your waiter first.) Many Chinese restaurants serve a whole meal of appetizers called *dim sum* between the hours of 10 a.m. and 3 p.m. (Consult the "I'm in the Mood For . . ." section for a complete list of Chinese restaurants that serve *dim sum.*) There is rarely a menu for *dim sum:* the waiter brings you the day's soups, pastries, noodle dishes, dumplings, and fried fare as soon as each is cooked. To order, point with your chopsticks. The tab is calculated by counting the empty dishes and it never amounts to much.

6. *Be Adventurous:* Don't overlook such "untouchables" as tripe, liver, squid, cusk, or dogfish (shark). These foods are regarded as delicacies in many parts of the world and their preparation actually requires more care than such popular items as lobster and steak.

7. *Know When Not To Be Cheap:* Namely, when it comes time for tipping. (For a complete guide to tipping, see pages 154–155.) Good service can vastly improve an indifferent meal while bad service can ruin the most splendid cooking. A serving person remembers past generosity and is quick to reward it with continued good service.

157

THE CRITIC'S CHOICE

Four-Star Restaurants

L'Espalier
Panache
Chillingsworth
Apley's

Three-and-a-half-Star Restaurants

Julien at the Hotel Meridien
Allegro
Upstairs at the Pudding
Seasons Restaurant
Locke-Ober's
The Harvest Restaurant

An All-Star Lineup of Steven Raichlen's Favorite Restaurants

Allegro
Bangkok Cuisine
Buteco
Daily Catch
Ho Yuen Ting
Korea House
L'Espalier
Mandalay
Panache
Sol Azteca

INDEX OF RESTAURANTS